The Ecu Report

The Ecu Report

*Michael Emerson and
Christopher Huhne*

Pan Books
in association with
Sidgwick & Jackson

First published in Great Britain in 1991 by
Pan Books Ltd, Cavaye Place, London SW10 9PG
in association with
Sidgwick & Jackson Limited

9 8 7 6 5 4 3 2 1

ISBN 0 330 32186 2

Photoset by Parker Typesetting Service, Leicester

Printed in England by Clays Ltd, St Ives plc

Contents

List of numbered figures and tables

Foreword

Economic and Monetary Union (EMU) would be the step which would do more to affect ordinary people's lives than anything else on the menu in Brussels. This book therefore sets out to explain the issues involved in moving towards a single European currency. It lays some old canards to rest, and it addresses some concerns and fears which people may legitimately have about such a considerable move. Most of all, it aims to demystify the mysterious by ensuring that no intelligent reader feels that they are being blinded by science. EMU is one of those economic issues which is far too important to be ignored by citizens. It is also a political affair.

If you are not a European, read about the ecu with care, for it will be a world currency to rival the dollar and the yen. After several previous attempts, the signs are that the time is now ripe and that Europe will adopt its own currency. The Community itself has a new self-confidence. That *élan* has been born out of a successful settlement of earlier disputes and, even more importantly, out of the success of the 1992 programme to create a genuinely integrated, single European market. Economic and monetary union – a single currency for Europe – is logically the next big step on the agenda.

Let us briefly recall the recent origins of this move to EMU. In 1988, our twelve heads of state and government decided to commission a report into how an economic and monetary union might be attained. That report, the product of a committee of Europe's central bankers and some independent monetary experts under the chairmanship of President Delors, proposed a framework for economic and monetary union based on the principles of parallelism and subsidiarity: there has to be a parallel development on the economic and the monetary side. Also it has to be ensured that only those powers which have to be centralised are transferred from national to Community level.

The process involves three stages: stage one would involve all Community currencies participating in the exchange rate mechanism of the European Monetary System; stage two would involve the setting up of a system of European central banks to run EMU; stage three would involve locking together the national currencies or adopting a single currency.

Operationally, the Community began its renewed moves towards Economic and Monetary Union on 1 July 1990, which was the point at which the heads of state and government agreed stage one of the process proposed in the committee report should begin. With the participation now of Spain and the United Kingdom alongside the eight original member countries of the European Monetary System, more than 90 per cent of the Community economy is now managed under the influence of a powerful mechanism of monetary policy co-ordination. This must be a good augury for the further progess sought in bringing the performance of the Community's economies into line during stage one.

These developments cannot take place without modification to the Treaty of Rome, the Community's constitution. In December 1990, the twelve member states of the Community opened two intergovernmental conferences to negotiate the treaty changes which are necessary for economic and monetary union and so-called political union. It has been decided that these negotiations should be concluded in good time for the full ratification of the Treaty to take place by 1 January 1993.

The Community's agenda is thus clear, and it is of historic importance not only to the existing member states of the Community but also to those countries which are applying for membership. Clearly, there are both political and economic elements to what is proposed. But the whole process of further integration depends on the implications of economic and monetary union.

This is why the Commission decided to prepare a thorough

economic appraisal of the likely economic effects · well as benefits – of the move to EMU. The idea was bridge between the policy makers on one hand and the community of academic economists on the other, so that there could be a fruitful two-way flow of ideas, research and advice. The findings of that research programme were, however, published in two heavy and rather technical volumes. The objective of this book by Michael Emerson, the distinguished director of the study, and Christopher Huhne, a leading economic journalist, is to make the findings available to a wide audience in the member states and beyond.

Both the study and the book are in many ways a sequel to the research into the economics of 1992 which the Commission published in 1988. That study helped to clarify the Commission's objectives and priorities, and it also helped to establish the credibility of the 1992 programme in the eyes of business opinion. The whole process was so successful that the pain of restructuring which the study anticipated for the early years of the single market did not occur: instead, businesses have anticipated solid growth, and have hence brought forward many of their investment plans.

No study can resolve all the uncertainties which surround a project as radical as EMU, but this volume does offer a handbook on the economic implications of the possible choices ahead for the member states and the Community. Consumers, investors, trade unions and businesses are offered a map to the sometimes bewildering complexities of EMU. This in turn should enable them, as economic participants and as citizens, to understand the issues and to exploit EMU's benefits to the full while minimising its possible costs.

The onset of the Gulf crisis and the rise in oil prices, the economic problems of the Soviet Union and the Eastern European countries, the evidence of slow-down in several of the large Western economies, all presage a more difficult economic period ahead. How does this affect the EMU project? This book has much to say on this. It makes no attempt to discuss very short-run questions, but a pervasive theme is how best the European economy may be equipped to absorb major external economic shocks (such as an oil price rise) in order to minimise their impact. The central conclusion is that a unified European economic and monetary union can indeed lower the costs of such shocks compared with a poorly co-ordinated response on the part of national authorities.

The revolutions in Eastern Europe have also given a new political thrust to the momentum behind a single currency in several ways. Psychologically, they have broken down the mental barriers about what is politically possible. Only five years ago, some serious analysts still talked about Europe suffering from sclerosis. Now it is once again seen as a dynamic centre of the world economy.

The Eastern European revolutions have also raised the stakes at the intergovernmental conferences on EMU and political union, for there is a lengthening queue of possible candidates to join the twelve. The results of the conferences, which are likely to lay the foundations for a single currency, will become part of the *acquis communautaire* – the rules and laws of the Community – which new members would have to accept. The conferences may thus shape the way Europe eventually lives just as fundamentally, perhaps, as the Congress of Vienna in 1815 or the Yalta summit in 1944.

Jacques Delors,
Henning Christophersen
Brussels, January 1991.

Preface

The objective of *The Ecu Report* is to explain the key economic questions which surround the proposal that the European Community should adopt a single currency to replace its existing twelve. The book is based on the Commission's extensive research into the costs and benefits of a single currency, which is published in full in two volumes in the economic journal "European economy". However, we have striven to put into everyday language the inaccessible economic language of algebra and mathematical equations. The key arguments and evidence are nevertheless entirely contained in this book.

We do not promise that all parts of the book will be entertaining as well as educational, but we have aimed at least to make it entirely approachable. In order to help in so doing, each concept and term is explained in full when it is first introduced to the reader. There is also an extensive glossary at the back of the book. Each chapter begins with a short summary of its principal conclusions, and the main themes of the book are summarised in their entirety in chapter one.

Because *The Ecu Report* draws on the work of the Commission task force, which was directed by Michael Emerson, it is appropriate that we should pay particular tribute to all those involved in one of the most intensive research programmes ever undertaken into an international monetary issue. Daniel Gros and Jean Pisani-Ferry made a major contribution, as did Horst Reichenbach, Alexander Italianer, Stefan Lehner and Marc Vanheukelen. The computer modelling work was undertaken by Jean Pisani-Ferry, Alexander Italianer and Andries Brandsma. The research on the costs of exchanging one currency for another was undertaken by Marc Vanheukelen. Valuable contributions were also made by officials outside the directorate immediately concerned, notably Jorge Braga de Macedo, Joan Pearce, Juergen Kroeger, Antonio Cabral, Pedro Santos and Christian Ghymers. The task force also benefited from the advice of Antonio Costa, Giovanni Ravasio, Heinrich Matthes, Jean-François Pons and Herve Carre.

Several academic economists also gave useful advice, including Michel Aglietta, Richard Baldwin, Peter Bofinger, Anton Brender, Ralph Bryant, Jean-Michel Charpin, Alex Cukierman, Andrew Hughes-Hallet, Peter Kenen, Willem Molle, Manfred Neumann, Richard Portes, Andre Sapir, Niels Thygesen, Frederik van der Ploeg, Paul Van Rompuy and Charles Wyplosz. Paul Masson and Stephen Symansky of the staff of the International Monetary Fund also helped with the use of the IMF Multimod computer model of the world economy.

The usual disclaimer must apply. Errors of fact and interpretation are ours alone.

We would also like to thank the publishers for their considerable efforts to produce this book in a timely manner and our families for putting up with the inconvenience of short deadlines.

Michael Emerson and Christopher Huhne
Brussels and London
January 1991

1 Introduction and summary

The introduction of a single currency for all twelve member states of the Community would be a dramatic and radical economic change. All the national currencies would disappear. Instead there would be one money – the ecu or European currency unit – which would be fulfil all the traditional functions of money in an economic area stretching from Greece to Ireland and Denmark to Portugal.

Imagine the implications. There would, as a tourist, be no need to change money wherever you went in the Community. As a businessperson, you would quote to provide goods and services in the same currency, knowing that what you received in cash would be exactly what you had planned, rather than a different amount determined by the movements of a foreign exchange rate. As a consumer, you would be able to compare directly the prices of cars or holidays or other expensive items. As a trader, you could take advantage of those price differences to buy and sell much more easily – and make a profit.

As a banker, you would be able to borrow and lend throughout the Community knowing that the only risk you were taking was the one you were qualified to take: assessing the creditworthiness of your clients. As an investor, you could decide to build a plant where the costs were lowest, knowing that its exports would not be made uneconomic by a sharp rise in the currency. In short, a single currency would transform many economic relationships for the better. But there are also less obvious costs in losing a separate currency. This book summarises the state of our knowledge about those benefits and costs.

One way of seeing the arguments is to start from what

traditional economics tells us. Here we have to embark on a little theory, merely because facts mean nothing without some idea of how they relate to each other. The traditional economic theory which can shed some light on the merits or otherwise of a single currency is the theory of "optimum currency areas". This hailed from a debate, largely in Canada and the United States, about the characteristics of an area which should have its own currency.

The theory recognised that money is a convenience, and therefore that a single currency is beneficial in eliminating the costs of exchanging it for another. These gains would be large if the country was small, because it would have to undertake many more foreign exchange transactions as a proportion of its income.

However, the original insight of the theory was that labour and capital – the two elements in production – must be mobile across the regions of the currency union. This would allow a shock to one region – such as a sharp fall in the oil price hitting oil-rich Texas in the United States – to be absorbed without excessive unemployment of manpower or machines. The Texans would, on this view, get up and move state.

Some enthusiasts went as far as to argue that the world's currencies were often not in "optimal currency areas": the western part of Canada and the United States should share one dollar because their economies are similar, while the eastern parts of both countries could have another; depressed regions like the Mezzogiorno in Italy or the north-west of England should have their own lira or pound which they could reduce in value against the rest of their country's currency. This would make their products – and their labour – more attractive to outsiders. It would help to reduce unemployment.

If this were the end of the story, the European Community would clearly not be an "optimum currency area". The savings in transactions costs, as we shall see, are relatively small. The mobility of Europeans is relatively low even within nations using the same language, let alone across language barriers. But it is not the end of the story. Subsequent developments to the theory make the idea of a European currency look much more attractive.

The most important failing of the simple view of an "optimal currency area" is that it implicitly assumes that reducing the value of the currency – a devaluation – can help price a country back into world markets. But there is a problem. The smaller the country, the less of its goods and services it can make for itself, and the more it has to import from other countries. When it devalues, it not only makes its exports cheaper, but it makes its imports more expensive. Its costs rise. If wage bargainers react by pushing up pay settlements, it may not be long before the rise in the level of domestic costs and prices has eroded the initial gain from the devaluation. Devaluation makes a country cheaper for a time, but it also pushes up inflation. It is thus more like postponing an adjustment than actually making it.

Within a large economic and monetary union, such as the European Community would be, many of the advantages of devaluation could be had without the inflationary disadvantages. The abolition of exchange rate movements within EMU would make it much easier to raise foreign capital to fund a trade deficit, an excess of imports over exports. This ease of external financing can fulfil the same function as a devaluation in allowing a country time to adjust to some external shock – such as a rise in the oil price.

Secondly, the likelihood and scale of specific economic shocks affecting particular regions may be much smaller than the traditional "optimum currency area" theory supposed. Old-fashioned trade theory supposed that there was a country which, say, produced bananas and another which, say, produced freezers. It then asked how many bananas would be traded for how many freezers given that each cost such and such an amount to produce. This, though, is a travesty of the real world.

All except the poorest Community countries have a very wide range of industries, many of which trade and compete with the same type of industry in other Community countries. This means that even a sharp worsening in the prospects for a particular industry or group of industries is likely to affect different Community countries in the same way. The implication of this finding is very important. It is simply that there is much less point in each country possessing its own currency as a means of lowering its overall price and wage level faced with some shock. Their common currency would be adequate to handle worldwide shocks.

Indeed, we report in Chapter 6 the results of an extensive study, using the International Monetary Fund's computer model of the world economy, which suggests that the Community would have been better able to withstand the shocks thrown at it over the last decade – including the oil price shocks, and the rise and fall of the dollar – if it had had a single currency. Both inflation and output would have been more stable.

The old "optimum currency area" theory also fails to take account of many of the developments in the analysis of inflation in recent economic theory. These have attached increasing importance to the expectations of businesses, consumers and wage bargainers. If people expect that inflation will continue, as they might if they continue to be faced with monetary authorities which have delivered inflation in the past, then inflation becomes more difficult to cure. As the authorities squeeze demand in order to reduce price rises, wage bargainers and businesses fail to reduce their price and wage increases. There is thus less money available to buy the existing volume of goods and services. Output and jobs decline.

If, though, people believe the monetary authorities when they say that they will reduce inflation, the costs of doing so can fall sharply. The credibility of policy commitments and the reputation of institutions is thus crucial. The Community now has the opportunity to build a monetary union around a standard of non-inflationary behaviour and credibility enjoyed by its least inflationary members. For most member states, this will have three effects: it will reduce interest rates because of reduced inflation and the reduced risk of future inflation, it will reduce the costs of curbing inflation, and it will reduce the costs of reacting to an inflationary shock like an oil price rise.

The old theory of "optimum currency areas" also fails to take account of new developments in the theory of economic growth. It is uncontroversial that the reduction in transaction costs will lead to lower prices for consumers and lower costs for producers, hence increasing economic welfare. But there is an important additional effect. A reduction in the risk of doing business abroad could reduce the overall risk premium which firms have to pay to raise capital from banks or stock markets. If the risk premium fell by a mere 0.5 percentage points, the resulting rise in Community income could be ultimately as much as 5 to 10 per cent.

This boost to investment and growth could in turn spark a more fundamental bout of business optimism, rather as the 1992 programme to create a single market has clearly boosted investment and growth within the Community. This optimism could launch the Community on a new and higher growth path permanently. Some support for this view comes from the remarkably bullish sentiments of business leaders towards the prospect of EMU.

There is a final category of gain which the Community can expect to make from EMU, but which does not apply to other monetary unions. The Community is a special case because it is so large: a market now of 340 million people with a combined income roughly the same size as that of the United States of America. The formation of EMU is bound to change the world environment. It will create a world currency which non-Europeans will no doubt want to use as a store of value and a means of exchange. This will yield some revenue to the European monetary authorities. Combined with the savings which could be made in the official gold and foreign currency reserves, thanks to the abolition of all the European currencies, the gain is likely to accumulate over time to nearly $700 for every European man, woman and child. In addition, international co-operation may become easier if it is conducted with fewer participants.

These are, in sum, significant arguments. The uncertain balance of benefits and costs of a single currency which emerges from the simple application of the old theory of "optimal currency areas" has gone. Instead, there is a considerable weight of economic argument in favour of a single currency for the Community.

Figure 1 A business perception of the microeconomic impact of EMU

Opinions on the prospects for the business climate become very much more positive
when a single currency complements the single market

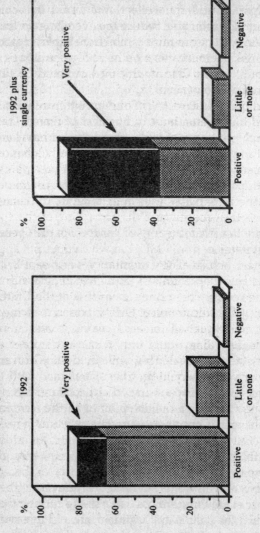

Source: Business undertaken for the Commission by Ernst & Young.

How fast could a single currency happen? The Delors committee – the committee of European central bankers under the chairmanship of Commission President Jacques Delors – set out three stages by which EMU could be achieved. The Madrid EC summit in the summer of 1989 said that Stage 1 – involving all Community currencies participating in the exchange rate mechanism of the EMS – should begin on 1 July 1990 but it set no date at which it would end. Both Spain and Britain have now joined the original eight participants.

During this stage, all Community currencies should be limited to a fluctuation of 2.25 per cent against their target or "central" rate against each other ERM currency and the ecu. (The European Currency Unit is presently a basket currency composed of the main EC currencies whose value moves in line with the weighted values of its constituent parts.) Because the same rules would apply to all currencies, this stage would also involve the narrowing of the special 6 per cent fluctuation margin used for the Spanish peseta and the British pound.

Stage 2, which all the member states except Britain agreed should begin on 1 January 1994, would only start to operate after the treaty committing member states to EMU had been signed. It would involve the progressive narrowing of the bands of fluctuation for each currency, and any change in their target value would only occur in the most exceptional circumstances. The fledgeling institutions which would run a monetary union would begin to operate.

Stage 3 would involve irrevocable locking of exchange rates without any margin of fluctuation. At this point, the Euro-fed or European Central Bank would take charge of monetary policy, including the setting of interest rates. This system of truly fixed exchange rates would subsequently give way to the use of the ecu as the single currency of the whole Community. At the Rome summit, the eleven agreed that the move to stage three should be reviewed no later than 1997.

Until now, we have talked about a single currency and EMU as if they were interchangeable. There is, though, some ambiguity about the terms. Economic and Monetary Union involves two components: economic union can be thought of as an intensified process of market liberalisation rather like that of the 1992 programme. People, goods, services and capital investment can move freely in an area where common policies ensure that there is free competition. This book, though, is mostly about the monetary part of EMU, and monetary union can mean one of two things: either it can mean the irrevocable fixing of exchange rates for all time, or it can mean the replacement of national currencies with one single European currency. The choice should be easy to make. The irrevocable fixing of currencies involves all the same disciplines as the adoption of a single currency, but it does not bring the same benefits.

Start by looking at the disciplines. Sometimes people imagine that there could be completely fixed exchange rates while different national central banks continued to be independent of each other, pursuing their own policies. But this is not so. If interest rates in one currency were higher than in another, although their exchange rates were fixed together, capital would flood out of the low interest rate currency into the higher interest rate currency. Locked exchange rates thus require that there are also locked interest rates: one monetary authority has to decide interest rates for the whole union.

How would the commitment to locked exchange rates be made credible? After all, several governments have made commitments never to devalue their currencies against the German mark, but it has taken a long time for their interest rates to become similar to German ones. Austria and the Netherlands are examples. In France's case, interest rates have still not fallen to German levels. The French continue to pay higher interest rates because the markets do not wholly believe their promise. Exchange rates are only likely to be deemed irrevocably fixed if all the official central banks in the Community guarantee to convert any one currency into any other at the official rate, without any limit whatsoever.

But this commitment also implies that there has to be a single authority. If there were not, any EC central bank could merely print money and force their partner central banks to buy up, at the official rate, any amount that people wanted to sell. It would gain from issuing currency, but would force the associated inflation costs on to other EC countries. Few EC countries would agree to such an arrangement. In other words, irrevocably fixed exchange rates imply all the disciplines of a single currency with a single monetary authority. There would be no room for decentralisation or differences in monetary policy. Although national monetary symbols, denominations and values might differ, they would in reality merely be different images of the same currency. The costs – the loss of sovereignty and flexibility – would be the same as with a single currency.

A single currency also has several advantages over irrevocably fixed exchange rates. The first is that a single currency would give maximum credibility to the monetary union. If currencies were merely linked, even with a firm guarantee from all the central banks, interest rates on long term financial securities repayable in fifteen or twenty years' time might still differ if the markets remained uncertain about whether the union would last. After all, so long as the national currencies still existed, it would be relatively easy for a country to opt out of EMU. The Irish punt, for example, had a fixed exchange rate with the pound sterling from 1921 to 1979, but it still broke it in order to join the EMS. A national government could also abandon a single currency, but it would be more difficult to do so. The credibility of a single currency would clearly be greater from the outset.

A second reason for a single currency rather than locked rates is that it would completely eliminate the costs for firms and individuals when they exchanged one currency for another. There is thus a gain in transaction costs. Because goods and services would be priced in the same currency, businessmen would be able to notice price differences more easily, which would encourage trade and competition. This is known as price transparency. Thirdly, some financial markets, such as those for government bonds, might begin to merge. This would make markets easier and more reliable to use for both buyers and sellers, and might lead to some savings by brokers due to economies of scale. (The problem with small markets is that sometimes there are simply no buyers or sellers at any price: they become illiquid.)

A single currency would clearly be more visible to Europeans than locked exchange rates, which in turn might make it easier to have some impact on wages and prices. If it is clear to businesses and trade unions that they are competing against the rest of the continent in the same money, they are less likely to raise prices or wages in an inflationary manner.

Finally, only a single currency could become a widely traded international currency and lead to a more balanced international monetary regime based on a tripod of the Japanese yen, US dollar and the European currency.

One common objection to a single currency rather than locked exchange rates is that it would abolish the national symbols and characters which currently appear on banknotes: Bourboulina, the leader of the 1821 revolution against the Turks, on the 50 Greek drachma note; the composer Claude Debussy on the 20 French franc note; the monarchs of the respective countries on Spanish, Dutch, British, Belgian and Danish notes. However, there is no reason why different issues of banknotes should disappear. The key difference, compared with national currencies today, would be a common unit of account and probably some common elements (such as size and symbols). However, the designs of banknotes could continue to be different, just as they are in the United Kingdom, where Scottish banks continue to issue differently designed notes from those of the Bank of England, although always of the same denominations. There are also differences between Belgian and Luxembourgeois notes, although the franc is the same. It would even be possible for the names of the old national currencies to continue. But one pound would be worth one mark, which would equal one franc, which would be the same as one lira or one peseta.

A single currency is thus preferable to locked exchange rates. The costs of adopting it are the same as the costs of locking exchange rates completely, while there are considerable further advantages. A single European currency is thus the definition of EMU which we will use throughout the rest of the book.

We have now defined our terms, but there is another

problem we have to set out. In order to assess the costs and benefits of EMU, we have to have some notion of what would happen if there were no EMU. In other words, we need a "counter-factual" or baseline case against which we can compare EMU. The present will not do, because it is clear that EC members are committed to measures, especially in the context of 1992, which will change the Community economy.

The natural starting point is stage 1 of EMU, or the European Monetary System plus 1992. The internal market would be completed so that there is a high degree of integration between goods and services markets. On the monetary side, capital markets would be fully liberalised. There would be closer monetary and exchange rate co-ordination. Realignments within the EMS would be possible, but infrequent. And all EC currencies would be within the EMS's narrow 2.25 per cent fluctuation bands.

This is a pretty tough basis of comparison for EMU, because it means that many of its advantages are already on the way. The basic monetary logic of stage 1 is similar to the EMS of the late eighties: it is an anti-inflationary system with increasingly fixed exchange rates. As in the late eighties, it will probably continue to be led by the German Bundesbank because its anti-inflationary policies tended to be more successful and hence less questioned by the financial markets. Its interest rates were generally the lowest in the system. If the interest rates of other countries were equal to that of the "anchor" country – Germany – investors would buy the anchor currency. So other countries' central banks have to set their interest rates above those of the anchor if they are to maintain their currencies within the bands set against the "anchor country".

We need to make one further point about the basis of the research before we summarise the plan of the book. This concerns the nature of the economics of a single currency. We have already seen, earlier in this chapter, that the existing theory of optimum currency areas is seriously flawed. The new developments in economics, though, do not yet provide an integrated approach to monetary union. They may never do so, because very different considerations are involved in different aspects of EMU. Microeconomic efficiency has little to do with the resistance of an economy to external shocks or with the debate about whether economic policy should be guided by rules or whether it should be changed with the use of policy makers' discretion. Yet all of these are important to any thinking about EMU. The best we can hope for is that hard-nosed research can obtain results which shed light on each individual area.

There is also a problem in pulling the results together because, as so often in economics, the theory and the empirical research depend on two different ways of looking at the world. The natural framework for looking at the gains which a single currency can yield to firms and people is similar to the framework used for analysing the gains from free trade: the classical microeconomic paradigm of competitive markets and flexible prices. This implicitly assumes that any unemployment of manpower or machines which results from such competition is very short term, or voluntary. There can be no long term problem of high unemployment or stagflation.

The second economic way of thinking about EMU looks at the costs of forgoing the currency as a means of adjustment. However, this only arises as a problem in a world where prices and wages do not react swiftly to changes in demand and supply. If markets are perfectly integrated, and at the same time prices are fully flexible, there is no point whatsoever in having a separate currency. In short, an analysis of the macroeconomic effects of moving from different currencies to a single currency implies a Keynesian paradigm of sticky wages and prices. (There is a fine irony here, since many of the right-wing critics of EMU are often those who are also most critical of Keynesian economics.)

In the present state of economic theory in general, and of theory about EMU in particular, there is thus simply no point in trying to reach an overall quantitative evaluation of the costs and benefits of EMU. The lack of a unified theory would mean that we would merely be adding apples and pears. It would not be meaningful. The best we can attempt to do is to indicate orders of magnitude for particular effects. Even this is not always easy. How could we begin to put a monetary value to the cost of forgoing an exchange rate in circumstances which have not happened and which may never arise?

We should now turn to a plan of the book, describing its structure and how its elements fit into the bigger themes we outlined at the beginning of the chapter. In Chapters 2 to 6, we turn to the main benefits and costs of EMU and we outline a total of sixteen ways in which EMU would change the Community economy; having enumerated the various costs and benefits of EMU, the three concluding chapters deal with transitional, regional and national issues.

In Chapter 2 we deal with a number of ways in which EMU would save business costs and reduce business risks, and thereby generally make the economy more efficient and dynamic. These are in turn:

1 The end of exchange rate variability and uncertainty. EMU would eliminate the variability of EC currencies against each other. The average monthly variations in individual EC currencies against other EC currencies is 0.7 per cent for those in the exchange rate mechanism and 1.9 per cent for those outside. EMU would also end exchange rate uncertainty, a more corrosive influence than variability because it is also more long-lasting. Variability can be abolished, but uncertainty can continue. The markets can require a premium on a country's interest rates, in order to compensate for the risk of devaluation, well beyond the actual stabilisation of its exchange rate. France and the Netherlands are examples.

2 The end of transaction costs. Overall transaction costs amount to some 0.5 per cent of national income (Gross Domestic Product), or about double the figure estimated by the Commission for the border costs impeding the circulation of goods during its research into the benefits of the 1992 single market. Transaction costs are particularly high – perhaps 1 per cent of GDP – for member states with small economies and a lot of international trade, and whose currencies are little used internationally.

3 Building on the 1992 programme. The Community economy should be able to secure further gains from liberalisation and integration, on top of those foreseen in the 1985 White Paper on the single market. These include a deeper liberalisation of energy and transport markets, which tend to be nationally oriented. On the public spending side, there may be gains from European infrastructural investments (such as better air traffic control) which would complement the opening up of markets.

4 Dynamic gains from lower prices and costs. Traditional economic theory has seen the gains from market liberalisation and from monetary integration as once-and-for-all reductions in costs and prices, which hence lead to once-and-for-all gains in welfare even if these are phased in over a number of years. But the 1992 process has shown how such once-and-for-all changes may also trigger an underlying increase in the rate of growth of the economy. As we saw earlier in this chapter, a reduction in the risk of doing business can lead to a rise in investment and growth.

Many recent analyses of Europe's relatively high unemployment have stressed the importance of inertia: once people stay unemployed for a prolonged period, it becomes progressively more difficult for them to find a job. A sharp boost in growth caused by rising business optimism may help to overcome the barrier.

In Chapter 3, we turn to the question of controlling inflation. We argue that it would be greatly facilitated by an independent central bank running a single currency. The main points here are:

1 The benefits of price stability. Over the medium to long run, there is no evidence that high inflation can be used to secure other economic objectives such as growth or lower unemployment. Inflation imposes costs on the holders of money, and on producers who have to update price lists. It may also raise the interest rates on government debt if lenders require a risk premium against future inflation which will reduce the debt's real value. High inflation also tends to

be variable, and to raise uncertainty. This makes price signals less clear, and impedes efficient resource allocation. It may also lead to 'stop-go' policies which disrupt steady business growth.

2 Institutional factors helping to stabilise prices. Any government can reduce inflation, but it is likely that the objective will be achieved more simply and with fewer costs by an independent central bank given the statutory duty of doing so. An independent central bank would have the incentive to meet its objectives. Governments have the additional objective of being re-elected, a goal which may conflict with that of maintaining low inflation. A European central bank – a Euro-fed – will receive the backing of all the member states only if it is mandated to follow non-inflationary principles. This would represent a considerable advantage for those member states without independent central banks.

3 The costs of reducing inflation. The reduction of inflation is often resisted because it involves a temporary loss of output and employment. These costs, though, arise because the squeeze on demand is not matched by a corresponding slowdown in business costs and prices. As a result, the given total of spending power can buy less in real terms. Output and employment falls.

If businesses and wage bargainers perceive that the central bank is set up in a way which really will reduce inflation, they are likely to alter their behaviour to reflect that fact. Their wage and price behaviour will be more moderate, thus reducing the costs of bringing down inflation.

In Chapter 4, we turn to the impact of EMU on national budgets, which raises both economic and political issues. The key issues here are:

1 A new framework for national budgetary policy. The loss of national monetary policy and the exchange rate will place new emphasis on the use of national budgetary policy – decisions on taxes and public spending. Budget policy will have to cope with any disturbances to a particular economy within the economic and monetary union.

However, this flexibility and autonomy must be circumscribed. It will need to be within a medium term context of budget discipline which avoids excessively high deficits. Although countries will no longer be able to print money to service their debt, they will have access to a wider pool of savings. A rise in their budget deficit would not necessarily involve any offsetting rise in domestic interest rates or the fear of a fall in the exchange rate as the markets worried about a trade deficit.

2 Direct influences on public spending and revenues. Central banks issue currency in exchange for goods and services: in effect, they can raise revenue merely by printing money. In EMU, the profits from issuing currency will accrue to the Euro-fed, but it would hand back these seigniorage revenues to the national governments. The only governments which might suffer some net loss of seigniorage revenue would be those whose inflation rate (and hence cash issuance) was particularly high. These losses could amount to 0.5 to 1 per cent of GDP.

However, countries with high interest rates will benefit as these fall to those prevailing in the countries with the lowest inflation rates. This reduction in nominal interest rates will tend to reduce the budget deficit sharply, although it will also mean that the real value of public debt is falling less rapidly. Real interest rates – actual rates after allowing for inflation – should also fall where there is currently a premium against the risk of inflation and a fall in the exchange rate.

3 Indirect influences on public spending and taxation. EMU will intensify the competitive pressure on governments, which may find that people vote with their feet if taxes are too high. In some countries, this pressure could lead to improved efficiency in the provision of public services, and in tax collection. Elsewhere, it could lead to the under-provision of public services and the erosion of the tax base, which is the economic justification for setting minimum standards of public goods or tax rates.

In Chapter 5, we deal with the main problem that EMU

poses, namely that of managing the national economy without the possibility of changing the exchange rate. This is the principal cost of EMU, and it is assessed as follows:

1 The loss of a separate exchange rate. The most important cost of EMU is the loss of a separate exchange rate against other Community currencies, but this should not be exaggerated. The ecu will still be able to move against other world currencies. Secondly, the participants in the ERM have already forgone exchange rate changes to a large extent. Thirdly, as we saw earlier in the chapter, a devaluation raises import prices and feeds through into domestic inflation. A fall in the actual exchange rate is thus no guide to the fall in the real exchange rate, after allowing for the difference in inflation rates.

2 Real adjustments in competitiveness. Changes in competitiveness – in the real exchange rate – will continue in EMU. Important prices like housing, energy, commercial property and wage costs will all continue to vary. The provinces of Canada have undergone changes in relative competitiveness between themselves over the last decade which are as large as those between the EC's national economies, despite sharing a single currency. Adjustment to changes in the world economy is essential, but the evidence of the last twenty years within the EC is that there is only a tenuous relationship between growth rates and the trend of price competitiveness. A strategy of persistent real devaluation does not appear to buy growth.

3 The reduction in shocks affecting individual countries. The case for national exchange rates rests mainly on the existence of economic shocks which might affect one country but not others. As we argued earlier in this chapter, the growth of trade in the same sort of products between the twelve makes it much less likely that a shock will adversely affect one country rather than another. Secondly, a credible independent central bank should reduce the risks of wage bargainers pricing themselves out of work by pursuing uncompetitive pay claims. Thirdly, EMU will eliminate the shocks which arise from a failure to co-ordinate international policies.

4 The increase of financial flows to finance deficits. The traditional balance of payments constraints will disappear in EMU. Governments have traditionally worried that if their imports exceed their exports by too much, the financial markets will sell their currency, and boost import prices and inflation. This constraint will no longer operate in EMU because private markets will be more willing to finance borrowers in the absence of a risk that the exchange rate could fall and reduce the investors' returns.

The final chapter dealing with the main costs and benefits of EMU is Chapter 6, in which we examine how the international monetary system would be affected. The main points here are:

1 The ecu as a major international currency. The ecu would develop as a major international currency. Non-Europeans would want to hold ecus as banknotes, which might mean a once-and-for-all seigniorage revenue worth $35 billion. The Community should also be able to halve its official reserves of gold and foreign currency, since there would be less call for intervention when most EC currencies had been abolished. This might save $200 billion.

The ecu's growing international role would also save European companies further transaction costs to the extent they could deal more frequently in ecu rather than dollars or yen. There would be an investment demand for ecu assets as the Community's financial markets became bigger and more liquid (i.e., easier markets in which to buy and sell). This could raise the value of the ecu compared with the dollar and the yen.

2 Easier international co-operation. EMU would effectively unify and strengthen the Community's presence in international forums. The reduction of the number of international players from G7 (Canada, France, Germany, Italy, Japan, United Kingdom and United States) to G4 (Canada, EC, Japan, United States) should make co-operation easier. The Community would have more weight in international bargaining, and would thus be able to secure a larger share of

its benefits. EMU could be a step towards a balanced monetary tripod of the ecu, dollar and yen.

Chapter 7 on the problems of transition argues that, since many of the costs of EMU have been paid, but the benefits have still to arrive, it makes sense to move rapidly to a single currency. There is a strong case for a credible timetable, if only because it would encourage wage bargainers to adapt to the new regime. It could also help to induce the sort of anticipation which led to the investment boom ahead of the completion of the 1992 single market programme.

Moreover, the increasing openness and integration of European financial markets means that there could be speculative attacks of enormous power on currencies whose authorities are perceived as being weak in their commitment to defending their parity within the ERM.

Chapter 7 also deals with the preconditions of monetary union in terms of economic performance. Monetary union requires virtually complete convergence of inflation rates. Nevertheless, monetary unions often sustain persistent differences in wage levels, reflecting differences in output per person (productivity) and competitiveness. The price of goods and services which cannot be traded – haircuts and restaurant meals – tends to be cheaper in poorer regions, reflecting their lower cost of labour. As they catch up, and their wage levels rise, so the price of the non-traded goods and services will also rise. As a result, they may have an inflation rate about 1 to 2 percentage points above the average. This, though, will not undermine living standards, since it will merely reflect their rapid growth.

Budget balances and current account balances will diverge even more than inflation or wage levels. The Netherlands has a high budget deficit alongside a large surplus on the current account of its balance of payments, whereas the reverse is true for Britain. Clearly, there is not just one possible pattern. The only essential condition is that public debt can be serviced without recourse to printing money – the option which would be excluded as soon as the Euro-fed became the central bank in charge of the ecu.

Of the existing ERM countries, Germany, France, Belgium, Luxembourg, Denmark, Ireland and the Netherlands are already similar enough in their economic performance to move to monetary union. The other large member states – Italy, Spain and Britain – are not far behind. Their economies should be ready within a few years. Portugal and Greece clearly have a bigger adjustment to make since both their inflation rates and their budget deficits are high. Even so, they could catch up with the rest of the Community quickly enough to participate in EMU at the outset, and might draw considerable advantages from doing so.

Chapter 8 deals with the impact of EMU on the regions. Its central conclusion is that there is no inherent reason to expect the poorer and peripheral community regions to benefit or suffer from EMU any more than the average region. The central regions have the advantages of being able to reap economies of scale by producing larger quantities for markets close at hand, but it is not obvious that this advantage is set to grow. The poorer regions also have advantages, notably lower labour costs. If the removal of exchange rate uncertainty unleashes an investment boom, the poorer regions might expect to benefit disproportionately.

Chapter 9 looks at particular costs and benefits for each member state, and at the views of the leading participants in the policy debate within each of them.

Overall, EMU is a particularly difficult change to assess. There are no obvious historical precedents for a monetary union of so many different nationalities. Moreover, it is not the sort of small step which economists like to try to assess: we can imagine, say, raising the basic income tax rate by 1 per cent and envisage that the world will be little changed as a result. But EMU represents an enormous change in the whole system of economic management, affecting monetary policy, a new and independent European central bank, rules for national budget and the international system itself. It is thus a systemic change rather similar in magnitude to the decision at Bretton Woods in 1944 to adopt a system of fixed exchange rates.

Clearly, policy changes will flow from such an important

change in the constitution of the system. Monetary policy will tend to be directed to curbing inflation. There will be no easy way out through a national devaluation. National finance ministers will not be able to opt for excessive deficits to bail out failing industries or any other favourite project. Budget policy will have to be co-ordinated in order to ensure that common objectives for the European balance of payments or the ecu are met. There will be new competitive pressures on the public sector.

But it is also inconceivable that such far-reaching and well-publicised changes as the establishment of an independent Euro-fed could fail to influence behaviour. Economists are often sceptical of the quickness with which people react to economic events. Markets can often take a long time to reach a new equilibrium. But it is nevertheless hard to believe that businesses and wage bargainers would ignore the fact that such an important part of overall economic policy – monetary policy – had a sign hung out saying "Under new management".

All of these changes – systemic changes, policy changes and behavioural changes – ultimately bear down on the classic objectives of economic policy making: efficiency, stability and equity. A single currency would make the European market work better, and deliver more prosperity. It would therefore be efficient. EMU would set up a framework which made the European economic system less prone to volatile inflation or output. It would therefore be stable. The only question mark is over equity. Would the poorer regions benefit more? Economic theory is inconclusive. Economic history, though, suggests that the poorer regions do best when growth is high throughout the economy. It would be surprising if EMU did not deliver equity as well.

2 The gains in efficiency and growth

Summary

This chapter looks at what would happen to the economic efficiency of the private sector – businesses and households – as a result of economic union and a single currency. Economic efficiency does not necessarily mean the production of something using the most highly advanced and expensive equipment, which might be the scientific definition. Economic or "allocative" efficiency means the production of the combination of goods and services which people want by means of the lowest cost combination of labour, capital and land. The gains in efficiency made by the public sector are discussed in Chapters 5 and 7.

The main findings of this chapter are:

1 A single currency would eliminate the present costs of converting one EC currency into another. The savings in transaction costs would be more than 15 billion ecu each year, or about 0.4 per cent of Community output (Gross Domestic Product or GDP). Most of these gains are financial, and consist of the disappearance of bank commissions and of the exchange margin or "spread" by which a bank sells a currency more expensively than it purchases it. Firms can also save costs. Many large firms run Treasury departments which manage their currencies.

2 Transaction cost savings differ strongly from country to country. The larger member states have currencies which are widely used as a means of international payments. Their gains may be between 0.1 per cent and 0.2 per cent of national GDP. By contrast, the small economies of the Community may gain around 1 per cent of their GDP.

3 Transaction costs are more harmful to small and medium
sized trading companies than to large multinationals. Total
transaction costs incurred by firms amount to some 15 per
cent of the profits made on exports to other EC countries. But
these costs can double for small firms, particularly those in
countries outside the ERM.

4 The gains from the suppression of exchange rate variability
in terms of increased trade and capital movements are difficult to measure because firms can often insure against this
risk using sophisticated if costly foreign exchange market
operations. But business surveys provide strong evidence
that foreign exchange risk is still considered a major obstacle
to trade.

5 The gains from economic union would arise mainly from
better Community policies in areas where there are
Community-wide implications or big economies of scale.

6 A potentially very important gain arises because EMU
reduces the overall uncertainty which investors feel about
economic prospects, particularly foreign investors faced not
only with the inherent risk of a particular project but also
with the risk that an exchange rate change may wipe out the
value of future profits.

A reduction in overall uncertainty could lower the risk
premium firms have to pay to raise equity capital and would
greatly increase investment. Preliminary estimates show that
even a reduction in the risk premium of only 0.5 percentage
points could raise income in the Community significantly,
possibly by as much as 5 to 10 per cent in the long run.

7 By improving business expectations of future growth and
profits, EMU could lead the Community not just to a once-
and-for-all rise in income but to a higher annual growth path.
This would also cut unemployment substantially. Opinion
polls indicate that European business leaders expect significant gains from a single currency. The addition of a single
currency to the single market increases the proportion of
industrialists expecting a very positive impact on the business
climate from 10 to 45 per cent.

*

As soon as there is a single currency, all the costs associated with the conversion of one currency into another disappear. These costs take two forms. The first are the costs which households and companies pay to the financial sector in the form of bank commissions and less favourable exchange rates for selling currency than for buying it – the so-called bid-ask spread. Secondly, there are costs within companies which arise from the need to employ people and equipment in managing foreign exchange. Many large companies have their own Treasury departments, and some even have dealing rooms.

Take the financial costs first. They can be measured in several ways. The most direct is to count the income which financial institutions obtain from their foreign exchange services. A less direct approach is to determine the charges which banks make, and then to estimate the total cost by multiplying the charges by the amount of foreign exchange transactions between EC currencies. These data can be obtained from surveys of the turnover on EC foreign exchange markets or from member states' current and capital account receipts other than those in domestic money. The Commission used both the direct and the indirect approaches. They both led to similar estimates of the financial costs.

Using the first approach, the Commission collected confidential data on the banks' foreign exchange related revenue. Only information on total foreign exchange revenues was available, so it was assumed that half was attributable to dealing in Community currencies. (This is a conservative estimate, since the value of member states' payments and receipts in other EC countries' currencies exceeds those in non-EC currencies like the dollar and the yen.) The result is that banks derive a little less than 5 per cent of their total revenues from dealing in EC currencies. Since the banking sector accounts for about 6 per cent of Community GDP, this means that the total transactions cost savings would be about 0.25 per cent of Community GDP.

Let us now compare this estimate with the result of the second method: calculating the transactions costs from the charges and the volume of transactions. Bank foreign exchange charges vary considerably, depending on the currency and whether the exchange is immediate – in the "spot" market – or relates to some future delivery of currency. The size of the transaction and the importance of the customer also affect the charge.

The highest costs arise with cash. A notional example worked out by the Bureau Européen des Unions de Consommateurs (BEUC) in 1988 showed that conversion charges could eat up cash at an alarming pace. A traveller was assumed to start out with 40,000 Belgian francs in Brussels, and to embark on a clockwise tour of every community capital except Luxembourg and Dublin. In each capital, he exchanged his money for the national money at the advertised tourist rates. At the end of the journey, the accumulated loss was about 47 per cent. Table 1 shows how much he would lose at each of his ten consecutive conversions. The largest losses – 14 per cent and 21 per cent – occur when

Table 1 Currency transaction costs in a (hypothetical) round-trip through 10 countries

Exchanged on 1 March 1988	Exchange rate applied in local currency			Amounts after exchange transaction	In ecu[1]	Loss in %
B (begin)				BFR 40 000	925,18	
UK	UKL 1	=	BFR 64,95	UKL615,86	891,30	−3,66[2]
F	FF 9,8065	=	UKL 1	FF 6039,43	863,55	−3,11[2]
E	PTA 19,47	=	FF 1	PTA 117 587,49	843,69	−2,30[2]
P	ESC 1,18	=	PTA 1	ESC 138 753,49	820,35	−2,77
I	LIT 7,75	=	ESC 1	LIT 1 075 339,52	706,43	−13,89[2]
GR	DR 10,575	=	LIT 100	DR 113 717,15	686,97	−2,75
D	DM 0,98	=	DR 100	DM 1 114,43	539,42	−21,46[2]
DK	DKR 378,44	=	DM 100	DKR 4 217,45	534,42	−0,95[2]
NL	HFL 27,75	=	DKR 100	HFL 1 170,34	504,71	−5,56[2]
B (end)	BFR 18,14	=	HFL 1	BFR 21 300	492,66	−2,39
Total						−46,75

[1] Official exchange rate published in the *Official Journal of the European Communities*, 1 March 1988.

[2] Additional bank charges can occur.

Source: BEUC (1988b).

buying or selling weak currencies in strong currency countries. A weighted average of the cost of converting banknotes is about 2.5 per cent. Total banknote transaction costs probably lie between 1.3 and 2 billion ecu.

The exchange margin for travellers' cheques is smaller than for cash, but there is an additional 1 per cent commission. The currency costs of international credit card transactions are between 1.5 and 2.5 per cent. However, there is no data on the volume of either travellers' cheques or credit card payments so no estimate of exchange losses is possible.

Eurocheques are free of charge in many member states when written in the domestic currency, but the charge leaps to between 2 and 3 per cent of the total when the Eurocheque is written in a foreign currency. With about 40 million international Eurocheques in the EC each year, with an average value of some 125 ecu, the cost savings for Eurocheque users would be between 100 and 150 million ecu a year.

What about costs incurred by companies? Bank transfers have a high minimum fee, but they are the standard means of international settlement between firms. The Commission services gathered information on charges in a questionnaire to banks which suggested that the cost of buying or selling foreign EC currency in amounts up to about 10,000 ecu was 0.5 per cent. Conversion of an amount equivalent to 100,000 ecu cost about 0.3 per cent. Nevertheless, charges even on big amounts in weak currencies like the escudo and the drachma could still exceed 1 per cent.

Very large amounts, equivalent to 5 million ecu or more, involve costs of 0.05 to 0.1 per cent, which is the size of the spread between buying and selling exchange rates in the market which the banks use to trade between themselves. Allowing for the different scale of transactions, the Commission estimates that current transactions cost an average of 0.3 to 0.35 per cent and capital transactions (which tend to be bigger) cost 0.1 to 0.15 per cent. The overall average for the corporate sector is about 0.15 to 0.2 per cent.

In order to obtain an estimate of overall savings from the abolition of EC exchange rates, we still need to know how much turnover is involved. The survey undertaken by the

Bank for International Settlements in April 1989 suggests that the total net turnover on EC foreign exchange markets (excluding trading between banks themselves) is worth $13,000 billion a year. Some 34 to 43 per cent of this turnover is probably between EC currencies: in other words, between 4,100 and 5,200 billion ecus. Applying the average cost of 0.15 to 0.2 per cent, this would mean that the costs of exchange within the Community in 1989 came to between 6.2 and 10.4 billion ecu.

This is, though, not the total, because the BIS survey did not take account of exchanging banknotes and eurocheques. If these are added, we reach a grand total of financial transaction costs borne by the EC economy due to the absence of a single currency of between 8 and 13 billion ecu. This is between 0.17 per cent and 0.27 per cent of Community Gross Domestic Product, and is a very similar estimate to the one derived from the banking revenue data.

An alternative way of arriving at the amount of business done in EC currencies other than the domestic one of the country concerned is to look at balance of payments figures. This enables an estimate of the amount of capital and current account transactions for each economy. Unfortunately, the necessary data are not available for every country, so it is not possible to reach an aggregate estimate by this route. However, the data do show that some member states will benefit more than others from the abolition of transaction costs.

The greater the trade in goods, services and assets with other member states, the greater the potential savings. Countries with relatively inefficient foreign exchange services also benefit. And countries whose currency is particularly variable against other EC currencies would also reap disproportionate benefits.

In other words, small open economies with "small" currencies like Belgium, Luxembourg, Ireland and the Netherlands, or countries with as yet unsophisticated financial markets like Greece, Portugal and Spain, will benefit relatively more than countries like Germany and France whose currencies belong to the ERM and are also a well-accepted means of international settlement. The exchange transaction cost savings for the big member states are likely to oscillate between 0.1 and 0.2 per cent of GDP while the gain for the small open and peripheral economies could be as high as 0.9 per cent of GDP.

Apart from eliminating exchange transaction costs, a single currency could also help to cut the present expenses and delays associated with cross-border bank payments. In the United States, a coast-to-coast cheque costs a fixed money transfer fee of 20 to 50 cents and takes two working days. In the Community, the cost is far more substantial. A recent study by BEUC found that a bank transfer from one member state to another of 100 ecu cost on average more than 12 per cent. Less than a quarter was due to currency conversion. Despite the higher cost, the EC transfer generally took five working days.

The creation of a single currency and a single system of central banks will allow the banks' treasury management, accounting and reporting to be much simpler. When the technical barriers that still complicate the processing of international bank transfers are also removed, cross-border payments could become as fast and cheap as domestic ones today. There are an estimated 220 million cross-border bank transfers in the Community each year. The difference in the fixed processing fee between a domestic and an international settlement (net of exchange transaction costs) is around 6 ecu, so that the potential saving could be 1.3 billion ecu.

The existence of different currencies also leads to costs within companies. Businesses' accounting tasks become more complicated, so that more people need to be involved. Multiple currencies also mean that a firm's treasurer has to manage many different types of cash. This means that the cash earns less interest than it would if it were lumped together. Alternatively, the company's borrowing may have to be in different currencies, which means that there is a higher interest rate because the amounts are smaller. Different currencies lengthen the delays between debiting and crediting bank accounts.

These costs are difficult to measure because they are spread over so many different parts of any corporation. The sample of companies which the Commission examined suggests that the cost is at least 0.2 per cent of a business's turnover in other EC member states. Small and medium sized enterprises suffer more because many of the expenses are like an overhead: you need someone to do them whether 1 million or 10 million ecu is involved. The Commission estimates that these in-house costs amount to 0.1 per cent of Community GDP.

Table 2 Cost savings on intra-EC settlements by single EC currency (in billion ecu, 1990)

	Estimated range	
1 Financial transaction costs		
Bank transfers	6,4	10,6
Banknotes, eurocheques, traveller's cheques, credit cards	1,8	2,5
Total	8,2	13,1
2 In-house costs	3,6	4,8
3 Reduction of cross-border payments cost	1,3	1,3
Total	13,1	19,2

Note: Exchange transaction costs associated with several sources of in-house costs are not included in this table.

In sum, then, the total savings thanks to the elimination of transactions costs could amount to 0.35 to 0.4 per cent of the Community's GDP – around 15 to 20 billion ecu each year. This is composed of the costs of the conversion services of banks (some 0.25 per cent of GDP); the in-house costs of companies (some 0.1 per cent of GDP); and the reduction in costs which can only come about in international bank transfers if there is a single currency (perhaps some 1.3 billion ecu).

Against these continuing gains each year, there would be a once-and-for-all cost of introducing a single currency. The banking sector would clearly lose an important slice of its revenues, and many of the employees and other resources in the foreign exchange area would have to be redeployed. However, the banking sector is also likely to be the main beneficiary of the expansion of demand for savings accounts and other assets denominated in ecu, which would provide a growing market.

Let us turn now to a second, potentially large source of efficiency gains from monetary union: the elimination of exchange rate movements and hence uncertainty. This should in turn stimulate trade and investment. In order to estimate the potential gains, we present some data about the extent of the variability between the EC currencies.

We can define uncertainty as "any unexpected change in the value of the currency". Research shows that virtually all changes in the value of a currency in the short run – say, changes within a year – are unexpected. So short run changes in exchange rates are a good proxy for uncertainty. We will therefore use "exchange rate uncertainty" and "exchange rate variability" interchangeably: they both mean short run changes in exchange rates.

Do we, though, mean actual changes, or changes after allowing for inflation? Monetary union, of course, eliminates only actual (nominal) exchange rate changes. Surely, real exchange rate changes – that is, changes in the value of the currency after allowing for higher or lower inflation in the country compared with its competitors – are just as likely to influence trade and investment?

In this context, though, the distinction between nominal and real does not really matter, because changes in nominal rates are usually equivalent to changes in real rates for periods up to about a year. In other words, nominal changes are real changes. This occurs simply because national price levels move much more slowly than exchange rates. A reduction in nominal exchange rate variability is about the same as a reduction in real exchange rate variability and hence uncertainty.

What if these changes in exchange rates were in fact reflecting changes in underlying economic conditions? If most exchange rate changes were an efficient market reaction to changes in productivity, investment opportunities or other so-called "fundamental" factors, the suppression of this adjustment mechanism would actually lower welfare. But there is a lot of evidence that most exchange rate changes, in a period of free floating, are much more random. Researchers have so far failed to link exchange rate movements and any measure of the economic fundamentals. Currencies can "overshoot" and "undershoot" wildly.

There is a final caveat before we look at the possible gains from suppressing exchange rate variability. Any positive effect on trade and investment from stabilising EC currencies can only be considered as a benefit of EMU if there is no offsetting increase in the variability of the new Euro-currency against other world currencies. If, on the other hand, there is also an increase in the stability of the relationship between the ecu, the yen, and the dollar, then EMU will have an ancillary, inter-national benefit. Since the external and internal trade of the Community are about the same size, this could substantially alter the calculations one way or the other. This issue is taken up in Chapter 6. In what follows, we merely assume that EMU will not increase uncertainty in the global monetary system.

Let us now turn to the measurement of variability. The tables show the most widely used measure of variability, which is the standard deviation of percentage changes in monthly nominal exchange rates. The concept is easier than it sounds: you can think of it as an average of percentage changes. It is a measure of the degree to which a variable is spread around its average value. Table 3 (page 42) shows the overall variability of the Community currencies against all other currencies, within and outside the ERM. It also shows the variability of the US dollar, yen and the Swiss franc. Table 4 (page 43) shows the variability of Community currencies against each other, and Table 5 (page 44) shows the variability only against currencies within the ERM.

As one would expect, global exchange rate variability exceeds the variability of Community currencies, which in turn exceeds the variability of ERM currencies between each other. The effect of EMU can be read from Table 4, which shows that the average variability of EC currencies between 1987 and 1989 was 0.8 per cent per month. This would be cut to zero.

But there is a caveat. Clearly, the benefits are greater for those currencies which are not in the ERM. The benefits of reduced exchange rate variability for those within the ERM are smaller: the average change would come down from 0.7 per cent to zero. Much of the gain in reduced variability comes about in moving from a free float to membership of the ERM,

Table 3 Bilateral nominal exchange rates against 20 industrialised countries
Variability as weighted sum of standard deviation of monthly percentage changes: see text

	1974–78	1979–89	1979–83	1984–86	1987–89	EMU
B/L	1,5	1,4	1,6	1,1	0,9	0,05
DK	1,6	1,5	1,7	1,3	1,2	0,08
D	1,8	1,5	1,6	1,4	1,2	0,09
GR	1,9	2,3	2,5	2,7	1,0	0,05
E	2,9	1,9	2,1	1,4	1,5	0,07
F	2,1	1,5	1,7	1,4	1,1	0,07
IRL	1,7	1,6	1,6	1,7	1,2	0,06
I	2,3	1,5	1,6	1,5	1,2	0,07
NL	1,4	1,2	1,3	1,0	0,9	0,05
P	2,9	1,8	2,3	1,3	1,0	0,05
UK	2,1	2,4	2,4	2,5	1,9	0,10
USA	2,1	2,5	2,3	2,6	2,4	2,4
Japan	2,4	2,7	2,9	2,7	2,4	2,4
Switzerland	2,4	1,9	2,1	1,8	1,6	1,5
AV1	1,8	1,5	1,6	1,3	1,1	0,07
AV2	1,9	1,6	1,7	1,5	1,2	0,08
AV3	2,4	2,2	2,4	2,2	1,7	0,09
AV4	2,1	2,0	2,1	2,0	1,6	0,13

Note: AV1 = Weighted average of ERM currencies, ecu weights.
   AV2 = Weighted average of EC currencies, ecu weights.
   AV3 = Weighted average of EC non-ERM currencies, ecu weights.
   AV4 = Unweighted average of non-ERM currencies.

particularly in the narrow 2.25 per cent bands each side of the central rate.

What economic benefits could be expected to result from this reduction in variability? The main problem caused by variability is that it increases risk. Since people prefer not to be subject to risk, it is reasonable to suppose that variability reduces activity in any area affected by it – in this case, trade or investment for export. Given the delay between the signature of a contract, and the payment after delivery, even simple export transactions involve an element of exchange rate risk. Alternatively, a trader can insure against the risk by using the forward or futures markets. He can therefore know exactly how much cash in his own currency he will receive at some point in the future. But this "hedging" involves some

Table 4 Bilateral nominal exchange rates against EC-12 currencies
Variability as weighted sum of standard deviation of monthly percentage changes: see text

	1974–78	1979–89	1979–83	1984–86	1987–89	EMU
B/L	1,3	1,0	1,3	0,7	0,5	0
DK	1,5	1,1	1,3	0,8	0,7	0
D	1,7	1,1	1,3	0,9	0,7	0
GR	1,8	2,2	2,4	2,6	0,7	0
E	2,9	1,7	2,0	1,1	1,2	0
F	2,0	1,1	1,3	1,0	0,7	0
IRL	1,5	1,3	1,3	1,4	0,8	0
I	2,2	1,1	1,2	1,1	0,8	0
NL	1,3	0,9	1,0	0,7	0,5	0
P	2,8	1,7	2,2	1,1	0,8	0
UK	2,0	2,2	2,4	2,2	1,6	0
USA	2,2	2,8	2,6	3,0	2,8	
Japan	2,3	2,4	2,8	2,3	1,8	
Switzerland	2,2	1,5	1,7	1,3	1,1	
AV1	1,7	1,1	1,3	0,9	0,7	
AV2	1,9	1,3	1,4	1,1	0,8	0
AV3	2,3	2,0	2,3	1,9	1,9	0
AV4	2,2	2,0	2,1	1,9	1,5	1,4

Note: AV1 = Weighted average of ERM currencies, ecu weights.

AV2 = Weighted average of EC currencies, ecu weights.

AV3 = Weighted average of EC non-ERM currencies, ecu weights.

AV4 = Unweighted average of non-ERM currencies.

extra cost and it is only useful for deals which are likely to be completed within a year. Beyond a year, there are no developed forward markets.

It is, of course, possible to insure against exchange rate risk over a longer period if the company concerned is prepared to issue debt in a foreign currency. It borrows the amount it expects to receive in the future, and converts it now into its domestic currency. Thus it knows for sure what its receipts will be, and its foreign exchange revenues will be used to service and repay the debt. However, this technique involves high costs and can only be used by large firms with access to overseas capital markets. For firms located in small countries, the difficulties are compounded by the inadequate range of forward contracts.

Table 5 Bilateral nominal exchange rates against ERM currencies
Variability as weighted sum of standard deviation of monthly percentage
changes: see text

	1974–78	1979–89	1979–83	1984–86	1987–89	EMU
B/L	1,1	0,8	1,1	0,5	0,3	0
DK	1,2	0,7	0,9	0,5	0,4	0
D	1,5	0,7	0,9	0,5	0,4	0
GR	1,8	2,2	2,4	2,5	0,6	0
E	2,9	1,6	2,0	0,9	1,2	0
F	1,8	0,8	1,0	0,7	0,4	0
IRL	2,0	0,9	0,8	1,3	0,4	0
I	2,2	0,8	1,0	0,8	0,6	0
NL	1,1	0,6	0,7	0,4	0,3	0
P	2,7	1,6	2,1	0,9	0,6	0
UK	2,0	2,2	2,4	2,2	1,7	0
USA	2,2	2,9	2,6	3,0	2,8	
Japan	2,3	2,3	2,7	2,1	1,9	
Switzerland	2,1	1,3	1,5	1,1	1,0	
AV1	1,6	0,7	0,9	0,6	0,4	0
AV2	1,7	1,0	1,2	0,8	0,6	0
AV3	2,2	2,0	2,3	1,8	1,4	0
AV4	2,1	1,9	2,1	1,8	1,5	1,4

Note: AV1 = Weighted average of ERM currencies, ecu weights.

AV2 = Weighted average of EC currencies, ecu weights.

AV3 = Weighted average of EC non-ERM currencies, ecu weights.

AV4 = Unweighted average of non-ERM currencies.

There is also a more fundamental type of risk associated with exchange rate movements, which is that the business simply becomes uncompetitive because of changes in economic conditions (as opposed to its own incompetence). In other words, a particular plant or equipment can become unusable because the real exchange rate – the currency after allowing for the movement in the domestic price level – goes up.

A good, recent example was Jaguar cars in Britain, which exported a high proportion of its output to the United States. As the dollar fell sharply in the late eighties, it found it harder and harder to compete. In theory, it could have hedged the return on its investment over a prolonged period by issuing dollar debt, as we described above. But such hedging would not have made the plants profitable. It would have been in the interest of the company to take any profits made by hedging against a fall in the dollar, and still lay off workers and plant because it was unprofitable.

Very large multinational companies can insure against this risk by building plants in different countries, and changing their source of supply. They can also denominate their assets and liabilities in different currencies in order to reduce their exposure to any one currency's real movement. But in reality these techniques are imperfect, and very few firms operate on a big enough scale to avail themselves of them. The risk of unpredictable, large swings in real exchange rates would not exist in EMU or in the ERM since real rates move only through the slow movements of overall price levels.

What is the state of the evidence on these effects? There are a number of studies of the effect of exchange rate variability on trade, but they do not settle the issue. A big survey undertaken by the International Monetary Fund concluded that it had not been able to find a systematic link between short term exchange rate volatility and the amount of international trade (see IMF 1984). Individual studies which have found effects tend to have looked at the major floating currencies, where the degree of volatility is much greater than it has been within the ERM (de Grauwe 1987 and Perée and Steinherr 1989). Studies specifically on the Community have found only very small effects (Bini-Smaghi 1987 and Sapir and Sekkat 1989).

However, this may be telling us something about the problems of economics rather than the problems of currency volatility. The theory is clear: if trade flows are not insured in the forward markets, there is uncertainty, which will increase risk, and this will discourage activity. This essential home truth is supported by repeated opinion surveys of businessmen. For example, surveys conducted by the Confederation of British Industry have found that over half of all companies – and every single manufacturing firm with fewer than 1,000 employees – thought that exchange rate stability was important to their operations. Similar results were obtained in a Europe-wide survey for the Association for the Monetary Union of Europe. The "reduction in monetary uncertainty" ranked as the most important positive effect of a single currency.

The evidence of a direct impact of exchange rate variability on foreign direct investment – the decision to build a plant – is stronger than the evidence on trade (see Molle 1990). The estimates of a study undertaken for the Commission imply that EMU might substantially increase direct investment from one EC member state to another by reducing risk. Short term capital flows are likely to react differently. Some short term flows may disappear: for example, those associated with insuring trade against exchange rate changes. On the other hand, a monetary union should encourage the holding of shares and bonds overseas. After all, exchange rate changes increase the risk of investing outside one's home currency. A smaller proportion of savings funds is invested abroad than one would expect if it were in line with the distribution of activity and assets, and this is likely to rise with one European currency. European assets will increasingly come to be seen in the same way as domestic ones today.

One way of thinking about EMU is that it provides traders and investors with free insurance against exchange rate variability. There might be an additional benefit because interest rates would tend to equalise. This would lead to gains in efficiency because Community businesses would be put on the same footing, and would have the same undistorted access to funds. A study by Price Waterhouse estimated the potential gain at some 0.05 per cent of Community GDP.

Clearly, this is not a lot. More significant savings might result because of a reduction in the overall level of interest rates and hence in the cost of capital. The experience of the ERM has shown that even if exchange rates are fixed for long periods of time, the financial markets continue to exact a premium for currencies which are perceived to run less robust anti-inflationary policies than the German Bundesbank. Over the entire period from 1983 to 1988, the Dutch guilder has not depreciated against the DM. Nor has the exchange rate moved outside a corridor of 0.5 per cent, well within the notional 2.25 per cent bands. But the three month interest rate on guilders has on average been 0.05 per cent higher than the comparable DM rate. A fall in the average EC interest rate would have substantial beneficial effects on investment and the economy.

There are also likely to be efficiency gains from the economic part of EMU, which essentially involves the completion of the 1992 programme. These gains have already been enumerated in the Cecchini report, which found that the creation of a single European market could lead to welfare gains worth 4.25 to 6.5 per cent of Community GDP.

But the Commission is now intending to take action which goes further than the 1985 White Paper, notably in energy and transport. The long term gains from a free internal energy market in electricity are now put at 11 billion ecu against 6 billion ecu estimated in the Cecchini report. The benefits of airline competition are now estimated at double those found by Cecchini. The most obvious area of activity which might be intensified by EMU is competition policy. With EMU, the need to restrict state subsidies increases simply because it is no longer possible to compensate for the overall level of aid by means of a change in the exchange rate. The gains from phasing out state aids would be large. For example, a recent study of Germany suggested that its GDP could be 0.9 per cent higher if aids were abolished.

So far in this chapter, we have looked at gains which are likely to have a once-and-for-all effect on the Community economy, such as a further reduction in barriers to trade which might come about as the 1992 programme is completed, or a cut in overall interest rates, or an equalisation of the terms on which finance is available to EC companies.

But it is also likely that these advantages will lead to additional indirect gains, which we can call "dynamic" gains because they would increase the stock of capital and hence potential output. This happens through a very simple mechanism. We have seen that there are gains in efficiency due to a single currency. These mean that more output can be produced with a given stock of capital. That in turn means that capital investment becomes more attractive because its cost has stayed the same, but its returns have risen. Capital investment will therefore rise.

We can call this, after Baldwin (1990), the "medium run

growth bonus". In the context of the 1992 programme, Baldwin estimates that the medium run bonus may range between 24 per cent and 136 per cent of the initial gains in efficiency arising from the reduction in trade barriers.

This would clearly make a substantial difference to the Community's economic performance. The build-up of production capacity could well take several years. Baldwin expects half of the growth bonus to take around ten years to occur. If the initial efficiency gains due to the completion of the internal EC market take about the same amount of time, we could be looking at an increase in the Community growth rate of two thirds of a percentage point for a decade and of a quarter of a percentage point thereafter.

Table 6 The medium-run growth bonus as a percentage of static efficiency gains

	B	D	F	NL	UK	Average
Low estimate	38	36	30	35	24	32,6
High estimate	136	129	80	124	93	112,4

Source: Baldwin (1989)

Is this plausible? Clearly, we are in an extremely tentative area here. There are no certainties.. But there has been a noticeable investment boom in the European economies as a result of the 1992 programme, which gives some confidence that such efficiency gains do occur. Indeed, the Commission's Cecchini report projected that the gains would only arrive after a period of competitive adjustment. However, the programme instead appears to have boosted business confidence and investment immediately.

There must, though, be a caveat. The efficiency gains are an unalloyed advantage. You can think of them as manna from heaven, materialising out of thin air. They require no increase in investment or hard work: it is merely that everything works more smoothly. However, the growth bonus only comes about if the Community economy steps up its investment. In order to do that, it has to set aside real resources for capital equipment which might otherwise be used for consumption. Unlike the efficiency gains which result from EMU, the growth bonus has to be earned.

So far, we have looked at economic effects which have been extensively analysed in the mainstream economics literature, and about which we can be fairly confident. However, the standard economic theory of growth – the so-called 'neo-classical' theory – has distinct drawbacks as an explanation of the real world. It can only explain continuing economic growth if it is assumed that there are continuing technical innovations: new products and new processes. However, growth appears, historically, to have been more sustained than this would imply.

One possibility is that a key assumption of the neo-classical theory – that the returns on an investment are similar whether the investment is large or small – is simply wrong. If there are increasing returns for big investments, then it becomes possible to explain growth without thinking merely about new technology. Growth can come about because people decide to exploit existing technologies on a bigger scale. These so-called "new growth models" have been analysed by Baldwin (1989). He has concluded that, if they are correct, the efficiency gains from the creation of the internal market could permanently increase the Community growth rate by between 0.3 and 0.9 percentage points a year.

The same type of analysis can be applied to economic and monetary integration. Whenever gains in efficiency raise the returns on capital, the capital stock and output will tend to rise. Similarly, any reduction in the risk associated with investment will also increase the capital stock and output. What scale of effects can be expected? First, we have to estimate the gains in efficiency and the reduction in the risk premium, and then apply the medium run growth bonus. (The Commission does not assume any permanent increase, unlike the more speculative work.)

Let us first turn to the effect of the efficiency gains, leaving aside for the moment the question of reduced risk. There are two sources of efficiency gains: one from economic union and one from monetary union. On the first, the Cecchini report estimated that the efficiency gains from the internal market programme would be between 2.5 per cent and 6.5 per cent of the Community's GDP. On the second, we have seen earlier in this chapter that the efficiency gains from the elimination of transaction and hedging costs could be around 0.4 per cent of GDP. Applying the range of estimates for the medium run growth bonus already discussed, this suggests an impact of the combined economic and monetary union worth between 3.6 per cent and 16.3 per cent of GDP with a central estimate of 9.8 per cent.

What could this mean for the growth rate of the Community economies and over what sort of period? If we assume that the gains in efficiency are spread out over a decade, and that half of the dynamic gains are then released in the same decade, the impact on the growth of GDP could be 0.7 per cent a year in the first ten years and 0.25 per cent thereafter. Given that the Community economy has a growth potential of a little more than 3 per cent a year, these are big numbers. They are nevertheless based on the conservative estimates of the growth impact, disregarding any long run effects on the growth rate. A stab at estimating these, assuming that the new growth models have something to tell us, would suggest a long term effect on growth of between 0.4 per cent and 1 per cent a year. The Commission puts the central estimate at 0.7 per cent.

These estimates do not yet allow for any influence from the reduction of risk. The overall uncertainty affecting business might be reduced in two ways. First, there would be no exchange rate fluctuations, which could make a substantial difference to the assessment of foreign direct investment, as we have argued. After all, businesses are in fact neither able nor willing to hedge their foreign exposures fully. Secondly, there might be a reduction in the uncertainty surrounding the conduct of monetary policy, particularly in those countries with a less well-established reputation for fighting inflation.

The 'riskiness' of investment in real capital is usually measured by the so-called 'equity premium' – the difference between the rate of return on risky shares in companies and the rate of return on government securities with a fixed return, which are supposed to be riskless. This risk premium is usually about 8 to 10 per cent in industrial countries. It is therefore an important element in the cost of capital of firms. If EMU reduces the riskiness of investment, the risk premium will fall. And as the cost of capital falls, the demand for it will rise. Any increase in investment will then have effects on GDP similar to the gains in efficiency due to the elimination of transaction costs.

The main difficulty is in assessing the likely size of the reduction in the risk premium. Baldwin (1990) argues that a fall of up to 1 percentage point cannot be ruled out, and that a drop of 0.5 percentage points is a reasonable central estimate. He also estimates that the risk adjusted rate of return on capital is about 5 to 10 per cent. If it is 5 per cent, a 0.5 percentage point fall in the risk premium would be a proportional drop of 10 per cent. If the rate of return is 10 per cent, the proportional fall would be 5 per cent. Productive capacity would thus tend to rise by between 5 and 10 per cent. The effect on GDP would be similar. Monetary union could therefore lead to very substantial effects on investment and output if it reduces uncertainty, which seems likely.

We have mentioned the opinion poll evidence from businesses in support of the notion that monetary union could have important effects on confidence, investment and growth. There is also a piece of historical evidence which is supportive. The last historical period when businessmen really believed that exchange rates were irrevocably fixed was during the operation of the Gold Standard before the First World War. As we might expect from the above discussion, capital flows across frontiers were much larger then than they have been since. The table, taken from a study by the International Monetary Fund, compares the average current account imbalances (and hence the capital flows needed to finance them) under the Gold Standard with what has happened in the post-war period. On average, the current account imbalances before the First World War were worth 3.25 per cent of GDP compared with only 1 per cent of GDP since the Second World War.

A number of caveats are necessary. These figures do not represent the total level of investment, but only that part

Table 7 Current account imbalances: Gold Standard versus post-war

Gold Standard 1880–1913 Average current account balance as % of GDP		Post-war 1965–86 Average current account balance as % of GDP	
Country		Country	
Britain	4,5	Britain	0
Germany	1,8	Germany	0,9
Italy	0,6	United States	0
Sweden	−2,7	Japan	0,7
Norway	−2,5	France	0,2
Denmark	−2,6	Belgium	0
Australia	−3,7	Norway	−2,1
Canada[1]	−7,7	Canada	−1,5
Finland	−1,6		
Greece	−3,1		

[1]Average of data for 1900 and 1910

Source: Tamim Bayoumi, International Monetary Fund

undertaken across frontiers. The figures for the Gold Standard period are even more suspect than modern ones, and these are net flows. They do not tell us how large the flows were in each direction, and they may have been smaller than the considerable gross flows today. Moreover, the whole theoretical argument that uncertainty curbs investment may be incorrect. There are even reasons in theory for supposing that exchange rate uncertainty might in certain circumstances benefit business. For example, a company might decide to export when it suits it, but not when it does not. Exchange rate movements might thus even add to its profits.

Nevertheless, this seems unlikely to be the general state of affairs. In Europe, where export markets are so important for so many companies and where the share of exports in GDP is so much higher than it is in continental and isolated economies like the United States or Japan, exports cannot be seen as an optional extra. They contribute crucially to paying the overheads.

As always, economists are able to come up with arguments in both directions, but the weight of the argument comes down strongly on the side of substantial efficiency gains flowing from economic and monetary union. Of that, European business is in little doubt, as the business survey undertaken by Ernst and Young shows. Ten per cent of businesses rated the 1992 programme as very positive, but 45 per cent rated a single currency as very positive. The single market programme unleashed a wave of investment in Europe. The movement towards a single currency could easily have a similar effect on business confidence and prosperity.

3 The benefits of stable prices

Summary

Most people agree that the European central bank which runs monetary policy in EMU – the Euro-fed – should aim at price stability. In other words, it should attempt to ensure that there is no inflation. The first part of this chapter argues that this single-minded emphasis on controlling prices is based on sound economic criteria, because of the other economic benefits which flow from it. The second section discusses the costs of attaining price stability. The third section looks at the type of monetary policy most likely to yield the benefits of stable prices.

The main findings of the chapter are:

1 Inflation imposes substantial costs, but these are difficult to measure.

2 Economic theory suggests that a continuing inflation of 10 per cent, which people expect and can anticipate, leads to losses of welfare worth about 0.3 per cent of GDP, which is a similar order of magnitude as the savings in transactions costs which would come about through EMU.

3 The post-war macroeconomic experience in the industrial world suggests that high inflation countries have a higher unemployment rate and a lower income *per capita* than low inflation countries on average.

4 High inflation usually goes hand in hand with variable inflation rates, which means that there is also unexpected or unanticipated inflation. Since unanticipated inflation can affect output temporarily, this also helps to explain why countries with high inflation tend to have volatile growth rates.

5 The costs of reducing inflation – disinflation – are mini-mised if there is a credible commitment to stable prices. Otherwise, wage bargainers can award pay rises which make their businesses uncompetitive and cause lost jobs. Similarly, the costs of cutting inflation come down if any linking of wages to prices – wage indexation – looks forwards to lower inflation rather than backwards to higher inflation.

6 A stable and credible monetary regime requires an independent central bank with a statutory mandate to guar-antee price stability. Otherwise, the public is likely to expect that politicians will boost the economy, temporarily increas-ing output and raising inflation. Such expectations can, in themselves, be self-fulfilling and make it more difficult to reduce inflation.

*

The economic benefits of stable prices are the obverse side of the economic costs of inflation, which is one of the most extensively discussed issues in economics. The debate has not yet come to any firm conclusions about the analytical basis for measuring the costs of inflation. As Stanley Fischer put it in a much read study (Fischer 1981): "It is well known that the costs of inflation depend on the sources of the infla-tion, on whether and when the inflation was anticipated, and on the institutional structure of the economy. There is, there-fore, no short answer to the question of the costs of infla-tion." He also pointed out that the inflation rate is not independent of all the other things going on in the economy – it is not an "exogenous variable" determined outside the economic system – and hence there is some logical difficulty in discussing the costs of inflation *per se*. It might make more sense, he argued, to discuss the costs and benefits of alterna-tive policy choices.

Despite these difficulties, there is widespread agreement among economists of all persuasions that inflation does impose costs on the economy. This chapter discusses the main elements of these costs, and illustrates their likely orders of magnitude with the use of some simple indicators.

Throughout the discussion, the term "inflation" is taken to mean a sustained increase in the general price level. It is not a rise in a particular price of oil, or of gas cookers, or of cars. It is a rise in the overall price level of the things which people and businesses buy in the economy. In a well-functioning economy where demand and supply are reacting to each other, some goods and services will always be rising in price while others may be falling. These changes in relative prices are not inflationary. Similarly, a once-and-for-all jump in the price level, due for example to the imposition of a new sales tax, should not be regarded as inflation.

We should first of all look at the effects of anticipated or expected inflation. Some effects are well established. Inflation will reduce the demand for money, because money loses its value. People will prefer goods instead. To the extent that the demand for money is artificially depressed, inflation thus introduces a distortion into the economy which has a cost. One small example: if you keep less cash than you would ideally like, you will probably have to go to the bank or the cash machine more often to top up. Standard micro-economics suggests that the scale of the distortion will depend on the amount of money in circulation but a reasonable estimate is that a 10 per cent inflation rate would lead to a loss of welfare of between 0.1 and 0.3 per cent of GDP. This effect alone is similar to the transactions costs which could be saved by a common currency. Stable prices are important.

Inflation may cause people to hold less cash than they would otherwise do compared with their income or spending, but the cash which they do hold is nevertheless shrinking in value. In order to maintain even a minimum reasonable level of cash, people are forced constantly to seek more cash. All the government has to do is to print the money, which it can then use to buy the goods and services it wants. Because there is effectively no cost to the monetary authorities in issuing the extra cash, inflation provides governments with a way of raising revenue like any other tax. Indeed, this effect of inflation has been called the "inflation tax". Much of the economic literature in fact argues that the inflation tax is no better or worse than any other type of tax, since all taxes distort people's decisions from what they would be in a free market. (The exception is lump sum taxes unrelated to any ability to pay, but these tend to be politically unpopular even if they are regarded as a good thing by theoretically minded economists.) However, it is hard to argue that there are strong positive benefits from the revenue-raising properties of inflation, though there can be important implications for the public finances to which we return in the next chapter.

Another effect of anticipated inflation is that it forces producers to change their price lists on a regular basis. (These costs are known as "menu costs", being analagous to restaurants having to change their menus.) In general, these costs are trivial.

But there is an important exception in the area of taxation. In most countries, income tax rates are progressive: they go up as income goes up. In addition, there is no automatic increase in the threshold at which people begin to pay higher rates of income tax when prices rise. The result is "fiscal drag" – the phenomenon whereby higher inflation increases the tax burden because it pushes people into higher tax bands than they would otherwise be in. This effect could be a cost or a benefit – depending on whether you are a government or a taxpayer!

So far, we have discussed the microeconomic effects of inflation. The macroeconomics are also crucial. During the sixties, the consensus macroeconomic view was that there was a stable relationship between inflation and unemployment known as the Phillips curve. The higher was inflation, the lower unemployment and vice versa. In principle, the authorities could maintain a desired level of unemployment by choosing an appropriate inflation rate. This view of the world is no longer accepted on either theoretical or empirical grounds.

The main theoretical objection is simply that it assumes that people never learn about inflation. If they come to expect that the government will allow an inflation rate of so much, they may adjust their wage and price expectations accordingly. By asking for higher wage rises at a given level of unemployment, they will cause the Phillips relationship to break down. This is broadly what appears to have happened after 1968, when the apparently stable Phillips relationships in most industrial economies broke down. During the seventies, most economies suffered an unpleasant mixture of higher inflation and higher unemployment which showed that there was no stable trade-off between unemployment and inflation.

Figure 2 Unemployment and inflation in the OECD countries (1970-85)

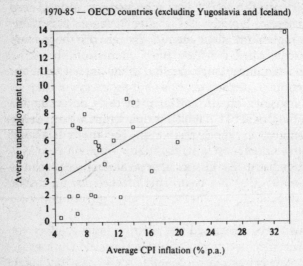

1970-85 — OECD countries (excluding Yugoslavia and Iceland)

Source: OECD, data available from 1970

Figure 2 is a scatter diagram of average inflation and unemployment rates for developed countries (members of the Organisation for Economic Co-operation and Development or OECD) over the period from 1970 to 1985. If anything, countries with higher inflation tended to have higher unemployment. This does not mean that the the reverse of the Phillips curve holds true. After all, there may be perfectly sensible causes of both higher inflation and higher unemployment, such as a poorly functioning economy. But it does at least suggest that higher inflation is not, in the long run, associated with lower unemployment.

A further indication that inflation does not have positive effects is Figure 3, which shows the relationship between inflation and the growth of national income (GDP) per head. It is apparent that high inflation countries tend to have lower growth of income, which is what one would expect if higher inflation reduced the efficiency of the economy. We cannot argue, of course, that this proves that higher inflation causes lower growth of income. Again, there may be a third factor influencing both inflation and growth. But the evidence is at least consistent with the theory that inflation reduces economic efficiency. Equally, the evidence rejects the sixties view that higher inflation benefits the growth of income. Statistical tests carried out by the Commission show that there is no significant relationship between growth and inflation.

Theory suggests, then, that inflation does not yield any macroeconomic benefits in the long run, which we can define as that period over which people's expectations have had

Figure 3 Inflation and the growth of real GDP per head (1955-85)

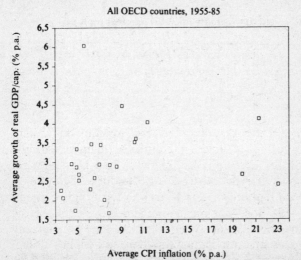

All OECD countries, 1955-85

Source: IFS
Note: except for the Netherlands, Austria, Italy and Yugoslavia, the period of observation is 1955–85

time to adjust and anticipate inflation. Indeed, the evidence is consistent with the possibility that higher inflation reduces growth and raises unemployment.

Up to this point in the chapter, we have looked at the likely effects of a steady rate of inflation that is quite predictable. But in reality inflation is never stable, and never entirely predictable. The evidence suggests that high inflation is usually linked to highly variable and hence to highly unpredictable inflation. This has been well demonstrated in the economic literature (see for example Cukierman 1981). It also leaps out of Figure 4. The figure plots the average inflation rate along the horizontal axis against the average change in the inflation rate (the standard deviation of inflation) along the vertical axis.

The link between high and variable inflation is also confirmed by statistical tests reported fully in the Commission's study. The tests suggest that a 1 percentage point increase in the average inflation rate is associated with a 1.3 percentage point rise in the average change in inflation. If inflation is high, it is also more variable, and hence more unpredictable.

Figure 4 Inflation and its variability in OECD countries (1955-85)

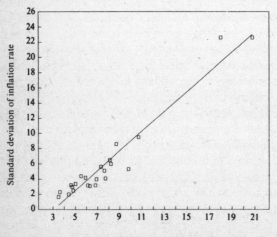

Average inflation rate 1955-85

Source: IFS

Unpredicted inflation has much bigger effects on the Government's finances than a steady, predictable inflation rate (and inflation tax). The reason a steady inflation rate raises revenue for the government is because people need more cash and have to provide goods and services to get it. The reason a surprise inflation raises even more revenue is because it reduces the real value of the Government's debt, which tends to be a good deal larger than the amount of cash in the economy. In almost all cases in the Community, government debt carries a fixed interest rate and involves a commitment to repay a fixed sum when the bond matures. A surprise inflation suddenly reduces the real value of the debt, and the real value of the interest stream payable on it.

Is this good news for governments? In the short run, it clearly must be. However, governments will only benefit in the longer term if their bondholders expect them never to allow a surprise inflation again. If the financial markets suspect that the finance ministry is going to condone another surprise inflation, they will merely refuse to lend the Government more money unless it pays a premium over and above what it would otherwise have to pay in order to compensate for its expected fecklessness. By raising the interest rates payable on government debt, the public finances could become weaker. This cost will tend to be largest for those countries which have a high public debt and a poor inflation record.

What of the macroeconomic effects of a "surprise" inflation? Modern macroeconomic theory holds that it takes time for people to adjust their expectations to a higher inflation. Thus a "surprise" inflation will tend to trick them into believing that the economy is growing more rapidly than they thought, and it will tend temporarily to increase output and employment above the warranted (or equilibrium) level. In other words, there is a Phillips relationship between inflation and unemployment in the short run. Higher inflation does lead to lower unemployment in the short term. However, the reverse also holds true: a "surprise" lower rate of inflation tends to reduce activity and increase unemployment. Thus it must follow that a high and variable inflation rate must keep output continuously away from the steady path of virtue. It must thus lead to losses of welfare.

This leads us to the key issue of credibility. Can people believe what their governments say? We have seen that governments have an interest in a surprise inflation in order to reduce the level of government debt. We have also seen that people are not fools: they therefore anticipate the inflation and require a risk premium. However, even if the government realises that the public anticipates the inflation, it may still, ironically, have an interest in ensuring that the inflation happens. If inflation is lower than expected by the public, growth may be lower and unemployment may result. To reach a situation where prices are stable and are expected to remain stable requires the public to believe what the government says. The public has to believe that the government will not succumb to the temptation to run a surprise inflation. Credibility is crucial. (We return to this issue later in the chapter, in discussing how the institutional design of the central bank affects credibility.)

A further reason to believe that inflation entails macroeconomic costs is simply the fact that people do not like it. In most countries with high inflation and democratic regimes which are responsive to public opinion, the authorities periodically try to suppress inflation with tight monetary and fiscal policies. The snag is that these policies are frequently hard to maintain in the face of rising unemployment, and the result is a stop-go cycle which can also involve macroeconomic costs because demand and output are destabilised. Figure 5 shows that a high average inflation rate tends to be associated with a more variable growth rate.

Because surprise inflation surprises different people to different degrees, it also tends to disrupt relative prices within the economy (Cukierman 1983). These changing relative prices, which are not justified by changes in demand and supply conditions, cause welfare losses because people are tricked into distorting their patterns of consumption and production. Estimates for Germany suggest that a 1 percentage point increase in the variability of prices lowers potential output by about 0.3 per cent (Neumann and von Hagen 1989).

Figure 5   Inflation and the variability of growth for OECD countries (1955-85)

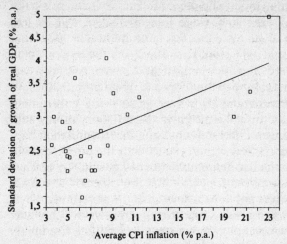

Source: IFS
Note: the observed period is 1956–85 for the Netherlands and 1960–85 for Austria and Yugoslavia (earlier years unavailable).

For all the reasons we have given, few economists seriously dispute that inflation is costly. However, it is another matter to argue that it should be reduced. Many economists argue that the costs of putting up with a relatively high inflation rate are less than the costs of attempting to reduce it.

Why should the reduction of inflation involve costs? The problem essentially arises because of the means which governments have to use to cut price rises: they have to curb demand by raising interest rates or taxes, or by curbing public spending. In so doing, they cut the growth of spending power available in the economy and put downwards pressure on price rises. The principle is the same in any market place: a fall in demand for a commodity leads to a fall in its price. If businesses immediately shaved their price rises, or if wage bargainers immediately accepted smaller pay increases, the slowdown in demand would rapidly translate into lower inflation. Demand would be growing more slowly, but so would prices and so would costs. There would be no impact on the real growth of output or on jobs.

However, if businesses and wage bargainers react slowly to the downwards pressure on demand, amd try to maintain the same pace of price and wage increase, there will be less money in the economy to buy the same amount of goods and services. Output will slow down and unemployment may rise. The speed at which wages and prices respond to a slowdown in demand is thus crucial. The more "sticky" or "rigid" they are, the harder will be the process of adjustment and the bigger the fall in profits, output and employment. (This is a traditional reason for advocating an incomes policy, which can help speed up the adjustment to slower demand growth without a rise in unemployment.) An associated issue is thus the Government's credibility. If businesses and wage bargainers believe the Government when it says it will reduce inflation, it will be able to speed up the process of adjustment, and minimise the costs in terms of output and unemployment. Once again, credibility is crucial.

The reasons for price and wage rigidity vary from country to country. They may involve backward-looking wage indexation provisions, or strong trade unions, or relatively uncompetitive markets for goods in which companies see little reason to respond rapidly to demand. Whatever the precise reasons for wage and price rigidity, there is little doubt that it exists in abundance everywhere. However, the size of the so-called 'sacrifice ratio' – the output loss for each percentage point reduction in inflation – is not constant. It changes over time, and it differs sharply between countries according to the flexibility of their labour markets and their institutional arrangements. For this reason alone, it would be extremely difficult to estimate the output cost of disinflation.

An additional difficulty in estimating the 'sacrifice ratio' is that it depends on that intangible quality of credibility. It may depend decisively on the policy regime, especially the exchange rate regime. The mere announcement of a programme of disinflation might not be credible, and might therefore lead to large output and job losses, if it is not backed up by, say, a commitment to exchange rate stability of the sort which existed under the Bretton Woods arrangements and latterly under the European Monetary System. A credible commitment to a zone of monetary stability such as EMS should reduce output losses, because it should also help to reduce nominal interest rates and have a favourable impact on wage bargaining. Certainly, companies in the tradeable part of the economy are likely to respond more rapidly if they know that the exchange rate cannot be devalued without the explicit consent of other countries. However, the evidence on the beneficial effect of EMS on expectations and hence on the costs of disinflation is not conclusive.

So far, we have suggested that disinflation will involve output and job losses unless the commitment of the authorities is completely credible, and there is no wage and price rigidity. Some have argued, though, that disinflation by means of a credible commitment to stabilise the value of the currency (within a system like EMS) could lead to a boost in demand and activity (see Giavazzi and Spaventa 1990).

Imagine a high inflation and hence high interest rate country which joins the EMS in order to pursue a disinflationary policy. If capital is free to flow across frontiers, the government's commitment to exchange rate stability will encourage an inflow of capital aiming to take advantage of its high nominal interest rates. Since it is committed to maintaining the value of its currency within the alloted bands, it will then have to reduce its interest rates in line with the countries with low inflation. But if its inflation only changes slowly, this will mean that its real interest rates – nominal interest rates after allowing for inflation – will actually be lower than those in the low inflation countries.

Its demand and economic activity will actually expand, and will lead to an increase in imports and a deficit on the current account of the balance of payments. This might continue for some time before inflation expectations subside, and real interest rates rise again. The deficit in turn has to be financed by the issue of debt or the sale of assets to foreigners, who acquire a claim on the future production of the country. The standard of living of the population is reduced in the future, even though its path of disinflation has managed to avoid any losses of output or jobs in the short run.

Others have argued that the flow of capital will indeed

occur, but that inflation would simply not come down in these circumstances (see for example Walters 1990). For them, the credible commitment to exchange rate fixity would merely undermine the fight against inflation because interest rates could not be held high enough. However, neither scenario appears to be correct. In reality, the disciplines of the EMS have allowed a fairly steady anti-inflationary pressure to be applied. Those disciplines have involved some costs in terms of output and employment.

Let us now turn to the requirements of a stable and credible monetary regime. The benefits from price stability can only be assured if the institution responsible for monetary policy within EMU sternly combats inflation. Clearly, an anti-inflation policy is necessary to curb inflation. But, as we have seen, a credible anti-inflation policy is also essential if inflation is to be reduced – and kept down – without output and job losses. Can Euro-fed rise to the occasion? Its success depends on its constitution, the politics of fighting inflation, and the behaviour of employers and employees. It also depends on the budgetary policy of national governments, to which we turn in Chapter 5.

Two constitutional features of the Euro-fed are paramount. The first is a statutory duty to assure price stability, and the second is its independence from political influence over its monetary policy decisions. Let us look at price stability first. Two issues remain open. What price index should the Euro-fed aim to stabilise? And could there also be other provisions in the Euro-fed constitution, such as a commitment to growth or employment?

We have seen already that price stability should be taken to mean not only an average inflation rate near zero, but also that prices should stay very near to zero at all times. The more unpredictable is inflation, the higher are the economic costs. The tasks of the Euro-fed should therefore be to maintain a stable inflation rate at or close to zero. The most appropriate index is ideally one which measures the inflation which imposes the greatest economic costs: for example, if inflation imposes its greatest burden by discouraging the holding of cash balances by consumers, then the obvious target index should be a consumer price index. But if the main cost is the variability in relative prices, then perhaps the appropriate index is of producer or factory gate prices. The consumer price index probably has the edge if only because it is comparable everywhere, and is widely used in wage negotiations.

What about other provisions in the Euro-fed constitution? At a general level, the greater the number of objectives, the less clearcut will be the institution's achievement of any of them. In practice, though, the provisions most likely to undermine the objective of price stability are the stabilisation of the exchange rate and the management of government debt.

If a central bank has to peg its exchange rate against other currencies, it may not always be able to avoid imported inflation. One country's rise in export prices becomes, with a fixed exchange rate, another country's rise in import prices. However, a decision about the exchange rate regime – whether the ecu should be fixed, kept inside a target zone or be left to float – is also of wider political significance. Arguably, it should be left to a democratically legitimated Community institution, whether the Council or the Parliament. This would be a similar division of power to that which exists in Germany. The Bundesbank pursues price stability, but the federal government has responsibility for the exchange rate regime.

Similarly, there is a danger to counter-inflation policy if the central bank has to finance government deficits. If the Euro-fed could be made to buy certain amounts of government debt, by issuing new banknotes or by expanding the money supply by other means, it could effectively be coerced into an expansionary monetary policy which could threaten renewed inflation. The Bundesbank could again provide a model. At present, the legal provisions in the Federal Republic provide the Bundesbank with the overarching mandate to secure price stability, but with a secondary requirement to support the general economic policy of the Government. The assumption is that if the two are in conflict, price stability will take primacy. The Euro-fed, if it is to be credible in its counter-inflationary policy, needs to have equally strong guarantees that it will not be called upon to create money to finance government deficits, or to subordinate its interest rate policy to the stabilisation of the exchange rate.

Even if the goals are clear, they will mean little if the Euro-fed is not also politically independent. Nothing could be more damaging to the reputation of a central bank than the widespread suspicion that it is subordinating its primary counter-inflationary objective in the cause of partisan politics. Yet the suspicion is widespread in countries where the central bank is not independent. As we have seen, a "surprise" inflation has the capacity to stimulate output, jobs and income, even if only temporarily. However well-intentioned policy makers might be, they would always face the problem of how to convince the public that they did not intend to abuse the powers at their disposal. By contrast, an independent central bank has no such interest and is subject to no such suspicion. Central bank independence can therefore resolve much of the credibility problem. It can maintain low inflation at relatively low cost in terms of output and jobs.

Economic research has tended to bear out what one would expect about central bank independence: there does appear to be an association between the degree of independence and the success of counter-inflationary policy. The degree of any central bank's independence is always difficult to measure, but some guide is the formal institutional relationship between a finance ministry and a central bank, the extent of formal contacts between the two and the existence of rules forcing the bank to finance deficits. These indicators were compressed into a single indicator in a recent study which then compared each bank's record on price stability (see Alesina 1989). The result is shown in Figure 6. It is difficult to avoid the conclusion that there is a strong link between central bank independence and price stability. Germany and Switzerland have the two most independent central banks, and enjoy the lowest inflation rates.

There are three key conditions in establishing the Euro-fed's independence. The first is that the Euro-fed should be entirely free from government instructions, whether given by Community institutions such as the council or the parliament

Figure 6 Central bank independence and inflation

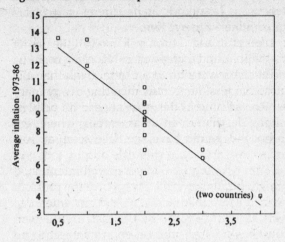

Index of central bank independence

Source: based on Alesina (1989)

or by national governments. The second is that its Board and Council members should be personally independent, so that no one could suspect that they might fall under the influence of other authorities. This means that they need a good pension, and may also need to sign an undertaking not to work for another public sector institution after their term of office. They should not be subject to reappointment by political authorities. The third condition is that the legal basis of the Euro-fed's statutes needs to be seen to be permanent. If the Euro-fed's charter could be easily changed, there would be serious questions about the durability of its commitment to price stability. If its charter is incorporated in a Community treaty, by contrast, it would have even greater sanctity than the Bundesbankgesetz in Germany.

Would such arrangements be undemocratic? The Euro-fed certainly needs to be independent, but that need not mean that it is unaccountable. The crucial factor is that its success should be measured against the sole goal which it has been set – price stability. Within that context, clearly its officials ought to be held to account for its spending and its policies.

There is no reason why its officials should not also be required to present regular reports on its activity in the same way as the United States' Federal Reserve does to Congress. Indeed, such reports could become a useful means of influencing expectations and increasing public support for its policies. If the Euro-fed were to act in such a way, its role would be no more nor less democratic than that of any other institution to which parliaments delegate powers. It would be a conscious political decision to set up an independent Euro-fed precisely because it would have signal advantages over the alternatives.

4 The impact on taxes, public spending and budgets

Summary

Economic and monetary union will have important implications for public finance, which this chapter sets out to explore. The first objective is to look at what changes may be needed in the way public finance is used as an instrument of economic policy. The second is to examine how EMU will affect the revenue and spending of national government or the structure of taxes.

The main conclusions of this chapter are as follows:

1 The challenge in designing the budgetary regime which should accompany EMU lies in reconciling autonomy, discipline and co-ordination.

2 The need for autonomy and flexibility in tax and public spending policy (fiscal policy) is all the greater because individual countries lose the ability to change the exchange rate of their currency against others'. Fiscal policy will become more important as a means by which countries can stabilise their economies and adjust to economic shocks which affect only them.

3 The creation of a monetary union requires consistency between the common monetary policy of the union and the fiscal policy of the individual countries. An unsustainable budgetary position could lead a member state to default on its debts or to seek them to be paid by printing money. This would be a serious threat to monetary stability. High and growing public debts would lead to pressures on Euro-fed to ease interest rates. The Community as a whole could be asked to provide financial relief. Fiscal discipline is thus vital to EMU. This is a live issue since some member states are

currently running deficits which are unsustainable.

4 An important question is whether EMU might weaken the incentive to run a sustainable, disciplined financial policy. There would be contradictory effects. On the one hand, participation in EMU is in itself disciplinary since it implies the acceptance of an anti-inflationary monetary policy and the renunciation of financing debt by printing money. The integration of financial markets may also lead to more sophisticated market assessments of national fiscal policies. On the other hand, markets are likely to expect that there will be some solidarity between member states, since solidarity is integral to the spirit of the Community. Equally, governments will know that substantial changes in fiscal policy will now have negligible effects on interest rates or on the value of their currency. On balance, there is no compelling evidence that EMU would adversely affect fiscal discipline, but there is a case for guarding against failures.

5 The member states' economies will certainly become more interdependent, trading even more with each other than they do now. Nevertheless, there is no evidence that the impact of one country's tax and spending policy on other countries would be so great with EMU that fiscal policy would need to be co-ordinated on a day-to-day basis. Co-ordination would be required if the ecu exchange rate and the current account of the whole currency area needed correction. Similarly, co-ordination would be required if the Community were to meet any objectives agreed with the Group of Seven leading industrial countries. In the medium run, national governments may be tempted to run excessive budget deficits because some of the adverse consequences – higher interest rates and a falling currency – will be spread throughout the union. Common surveillance of national policies by the EC finance ministers will have to correct any slide in this direction.

6 The "inflation tax" arises because people need more cash when inflation rises: governments can raise revenue just by issuing banknotes. In four southern member states – Greece, Italy, Portugal and Spain – the "inflation tax" is above average

because of higher inflation, greater use of cash, and bigger bank requirements to hold cash (reserves). These countries will suffer losses of revenue as inflation and the inflation tax falls. Assuming inflation falls from present levels, two member states lose revenue worth 1 per cent of national income, and two lose less than 0.5 per cent. Clearly, there may be political cost in shifting from an invisible tax to a visible one. The economic cost is negligible.

7 A move towards EMU should also reduce the cost of public borrowing in most member states. The present interest rates on long term government debt contain an element which is a risk premium in case inflation takes off, as a result of which both the interest and the value of the debt principal would be worth less. This risk premium will tend to fall as the markets expect low inflation to be the norm. Such interest rate savings will usually be larger than the loss of the "inflation tax".

8 The closer the community economies become, the more likely it is that people will take decisions merely in order to avoid tax or to increase their entitlement to public spending. At present, this is limited to some cross-border shopping in order to take advantage of lower VAT or excises. This competition could lead to pressure on governments to compete to hold taxes down. Minimum standards and common rules should be set when necessary.

*

Designing a good fiscal system is only partly a matter of economic efficiency. Economics can help identify those public goods and services – street-lighting, museums, defence and so on – which should be provided by national, regional or community levels of government if the principle of subsidiarity is applied. (The idea of subsidiarity entails taking decisions at the level nearest to the people affected by them, unless it is necessary to take them at a higher level.) Ultimately, though, a fiscal system is about political choice. Nor will this change with EMU. The fact that budget systems are so different in existing federations like Canada and Germany shows that debate will not end.

The purpose of this analysis is thus not to discuss what the Community's system should be in some abstract sense. We assume that the Community budget – which is currently limited to 1.2 per cent of Community national income compared with some 25 per cent for the federal budget in the United States – remains too small to have any significant economic role. Any budgetary policy measure – whether on taxes or public spending – thus remains squarely with the member states. The real question, then, is what are the implications for national fiscal policies of EMU?

We start by looking at the demands which EMU places on national fiscal policy, and we conclude that there are good arguments for national autonomy in a monetary union. The key point then becomes: in what circumstances does the fiscal position and policy of a member state become a legitimate concern for its partners in the monetary union? In dealing with this question, we draw a distinction between a concern for fiscal discipline, which is best measured by the sustainability of country's debt burden, and a concern with the appropriateness of the fiscal stance in the member states and the community as a whole. Fiscal deficits are seen as problems in the first case, and as means of influencing the economy in the second.

It is not an easy task balancing the Community and the national interest in these matters, not least because the timescales may be very different. The attractiveness of fiscal policy is as an instrument to tackle short-term problems (such as the rebuilding of eastern Germany). The concern with whether fiscal policy is sustainable is by definition long term.

This conflict, of course, exists even with present arrangements. But monetary union highlights these different time horizons. EMU relaxes the constraints on fiscal policy in the short run (because there is easier and wider access to borrowing at lower interest rates) but it makes the long run constraint more strict (because there is no longer any escape route in printing money to service the debt). However, even if the budget position of a member state is clearly sustainable in the long term, a change may still be desirable in order to achieve the right stance for the Community as a whole.

Let us look first at the need for national autonomy in fiscal policy. The most pressing reason for it is simply that EMU removes monetary autonomy. In the absence of a national currency and all that it implies for interest rates and exchange rates, what should fiscal policy aim to do? What degree of fiscal flexibility is required? Monetary policy would be directed at the management of the overall community economy, particularly at holding inflation down. Fiscal policy is thus left as the principal instrument for correcting the relative positions of different economies affected by any kind of adverse (or favourable) impact not also affecting the others.

Not all such influences need to be offset, and fiscal policy is not necessarily needed to offset others. We return to the issue of how economies cope without their own monetary policy in the next chapter, but the key is clearly the flexibility of wages and prices. Both economic theory and practice counsel against replacing wage and price flexibility by fiscal policy. However, fiscal policy can help an economy to adjust to a temporary change in its circumstances. Budget changes can also play a part in a medium term strategy to adjust to a permanent economic shock, in the same way as it does when a country has an independent monetary policy. Both roles are best illustrated with an example.

Suppose that an economy is hit by a shock to demand – a sudden rise in demand caused by households' desire to spend more and save less. Let us suppose that this increase in demand is large enough to pose some inflationary danger (as demand outstrips supply, and prices rise), and therefore warrants correction. With a floating, national currency monetary policy could respond by a rise in interest rates which would curb home demand and raise the exchange rate. The rise in the currency would cut import prices, which would in turn keep down the prices and profit margins of companies competing with imports. The inflationary impact of the shock would be small, and if savings rapidly resumed their previous level there would be little need for a further change in wages.

In EMU, the Euro-fed's monetary policy would respond only minimally to such a shock affecting one country. Its prime task, after all, is the stability of the union as a whole. Most of the burden of adjustment to the rise in demand would thus fall on wages and prices. The increase in demand would increase imports and raise the domestic price level. This would lead to a loss of price competitiveness, which would in turn offset the effects of the rise in household demand.

This process could well take time, which is why fiscal policy could be used to offset the effects. A timely fiscal tightening would ensure that prices rose by less, and that the subsequent adjustment when saving resumed its normal pattern would be less damaging to output and employment. In other words, fiscal policy could be used to help stabilise a national economy even within EMU. What is more, EMU reduces the disadvantages of fiscal policy. The exchange rate is fixed, and free capital movements make it easier to fund a deficit.

One way of assessing the effects of a fall in household saving in more detail is to look at the results according to a computer model of the economy. In this case, we report the results found for the British economy by using the International Monetary Fund's Multimod model. The model simulation is an attempt to reproduce on computer what might happen in the real world. It looked at the effect of a 2 per cent fall in the proportion of income which households save under three different types of monetary policy: a pure float in which the currency can vary against others; a fixed but adjustable exchange rate such as the present, first stage of the move to EMU within the European Monetary System; and EMU. The results are summarised in the three graphics. The vertical axes show the percentage rise or fall in national income (GDP), inflation (absorption deflator) and the change in the current account balance. The horizontal axes show the build-up of the effects beginning from the change at zero on the left to the eighth year on the right.

Under a floating exchange rate, the fall in private saving provokes an immediate 2 per cent rise in the exchange rate, according to Multimod. This is because the markets expect monetary policy to have to remain tight to counter the

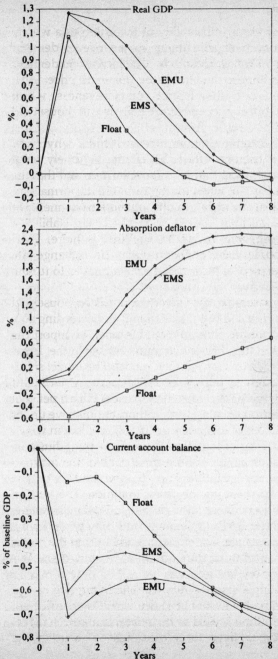

Figure 7
Effects of a fall
in UK
household
saving under
three exchange
rate regimes

Source: Multimod
simulations by
the Commission
services

increase in demand. The demand for exports is thus squeezed out, and the price of imports is lower than it would otherwise be. The expansion is short lived and inflation remains low. Within the European Monetary System, the exchange rate is only allowed to go up by 0.4 per cent in the first year. Total demand is therefore higher, and there is more rapid growth of output. After a while, the rise in domestic prices causes worsening competitiveness, and a deterioration in the current balance. Under EMU, the behaviour of the economy is not significantly different from its behaviour within the EMS. The interest rate and exchange rate effects are even smaller, so that growth and inflation are slightly higher.

The potential stabilising qualities of fiscal policy are borne out by the model. Within EMU, the fall in UK private savings of 2 per cent of income leads to higher national income worth about 4 per cent over the entire eight-year period. Inflation is up about 2 per cent. If the Government instead cuts public spending to offset the boost to demand from the fall in savings, the trajectory for both national income, inflation, competitiveness and the current account can be offset almost perfectly.

This is, though, a fairly theoretical notion. Most of the reasons which have led governments to use their fiscal policy to meet medium term objectives rather than short term fine tuning remain valid. Forecasting is difficult and prone to serious errors. The time delays between a change in policy and its results are variable and unpredictable. Unlike interest rates, fiscal policy is not easy to change. In most member states, tax and spending decisions only come round at a defined point once a year. Moreover, fiscal policy should not be used to delay market adjustments to reality when they are required. A systematic use of fiscal policy within EMU could merely swap short term stabilisation for a slower and more painful adjustment in the longer term. The only compelling case for an active fiscal policy is where there is a well-identified and severe economic shock which is specific to one country. An example would be the effects of sharp changes in the price of oil and gas on the Netherlands.

So far, we have been considering how an economy might adjust to a shock to demand which was strictly temporary. Suppose now that, instead of being temporary, the fall in personal savings is permanent. This might arise, for example, because of a cultural change which caused people to prefer to spend money now rather than save. What is the medium run impact of such a change? The economy is only capable of producing so many goods and services, so that a medium-term increase in demand must cause a deficit on the balance of payments (as imports come in). It will also cause a rise in domestic prices as companies take advantage of buoyant demand to boost their profits.

This rise in the real exchange rate – the value of the currency after allowing for the change in prices compared with other economies – helps to limit foreign demand for domestically produced goods, so that they are available to the home market instead. In EMU, it must occur entirely by means of rising prices in the area where savings have fallen. With a floating exchange rate, it can occur by means of a rise in the value of the currency, which reduces import prices and holds down inflation. But the loss of competitiveness – or rise in the real exchange rate – is the same.

Either a rise in prices or a rise in the currency will lead to external deficit, and ultimately external balance must be achieved whatever the exchange rate regime. The only question is how it happens. One possible mechanism is that there is a build-up of debt owed to foreigners, which eventually erodes wealth and disposable income, and leads people to reduce their consumption. This, though, takes a very long time. A second mechanism is inflation, which also reduces wealth by cutting the real value of deposits of money. However, it is not available in EMU because the deficit would not fall unless the currency was also dropping in line with the increase in inflation. A third mechanism could be a permanent reduction in the Government's budget deficit (or an increase in its surplus). This has the effect of increasing the total net national savings.

Two of these three mechanisms are weak or are circumscribed by EMU. First, debt is an uncertain means of reducing spending and the deficit. Secondly, inflation will be kept under control by the Euro-fed. With one means of cutting an external deficit weak, and another circumscribed, there would appear to be a rationale for expecting more reliance on the third: fiscal policy.

However, this may be wrong for two reasons. The means of cutting a deficit which is lost – higher inflation – is neither powerful nor desirable. In the Community context, it is not significant. At the same time, EMU should make the financing of deficits much easier because of the elimination of exchange rate risks. On balance, the reliance on fiscal policy may well decrease.

A related issue is whether it is desirable for individual member states to have specific fiscal stances. For example, one possible aim would be for each member state to keep its budget in balance after allowing for the cycle. In boom years, when tax revenues are large and public spending on unemployment pay is small, there would be a surplus. In recessions, there would be a deficit. But overall there ought to be a broad balance. A Government which departed from this principle would essentially be deciding to alter the pattern of income between present and future generations. A budget surplus – higher taxes and lower spending – would transfer income to future generations. A budget deficit would transfer income from future generations to our own. The issue is then whether such transfers are warranted.

A sustained surplus or deficit can be easily justified. The first depends on the nature of the pension rules in each country, and the size of the prospective pensionable population. In some member states with rapidly ageing populations (such as Germany), it may be desirable to run big budget surpluses in order to accumulate claims on the economy which can be used to meet commitments to future pensioners. A second reason for deficits might be the need to finance public investment which yield significant social benefits. This is a particularly important reason in member states which are gradually catching up with the levels of income elsewhere. (A particularly relevant case is the infrastructure investment required in East Germany.) It can be desirable for a government to run a deficit to fund capital investment if the capital stock is too low, and present generations are unwilling to reduce their own consumption for the benefit of future generations. There is thus no reason why fiscal surpluses and deficits should converge at any particular level within the Community.

We have seen that fiscal autonomy is certainly warranted on both stabilisation and medium term grounds. But this does not mean that any or all fiscal deficits are acceptable. We now turn to why fiscal discipline is a major concern in a monetary union. We also look at why fiscal discipline is a serious issue in Europe, and we examine whether the incentives to discipline will be stronger or weaker in EMU.

It is not easy to define or quantify discipline. The most straightforward definition is that a government is disciplined when it ensures that it does not become insolvent. On a narrow definition, this is taken to mean that a government should avoid any situation where its debt is rising more rapidly than the growth of the economy. Whether any government which fails to follow this strict definition can really be called undisciplined is a matter of later discussion. For the moment, we look at the consequences of the strict definition.

Budgetary sustainability must always be a concern for monetary authorities – including the Euro-fed – simply because budgetary and monetary policy are interlinked. In the long run, protracted deficits leading to unsustainable debts end up with governments printing money or defaulting. In either case, the monetary authorities must be concerned. In the first, they undermine their counter-inflationary objectives. In the second, a key asset underlying the financial system becomes worthless, exposing the whole network of financial relationships.

Nor are the dangers entirely of a long term kind. Unsustainable budgets would have shorter term effects on other members of the community. They might inhibit the Euro-fed from necessary monetary tightening simply because of the likely effects on tax revenues and budgets. If the markets suspect that the central bank is tempted to resort to inflation to alleviate a budget problem, there will be a loss to its own credibility and a rise in the element of interest rates which represents a risk premium for future inflation.

Even if there is no impact on the Euro-fed, an unsustainable budget position could easily have an impact on other member states. Their interest rates would tend to rise to reflect the perceived risk that countries could default, without being bailed out by other members, or could drop out of the EMU altogether in order to print national currency to service the debt. In other words, there are plenty of reasons to suppose that public deficits and debts would legitimately be a cause for concern for all the member states, simply because of their interdependence.

So far, we have looked at unsustainable deficits on the narrow definition which implies that debt is growing more rapidly than income. Could even sustainable deficits – on this definition – in fact prove to be excessive because they would have damaging effects on the Community? One example might be if a member state ran a large current account deficit because of high spending (or low savings). This could provoke some rise in the common interest rate on ecus, an external deficit for the Community as a whole, and a rise in the ecu exchange rate against the dollar and the yen. The interest of the Community might dictate a reduction in the country's budget deficit in order to curb demand and the current account deficit. The same thing could happen in reverse, and there is really no way of predicting in advance all the circumstances in which policies may prove to be inappropriate. Regular policy co-ordination, through the monthly meetings of the Economic and Finance ministers, is the only way to address the problem.

Sadly, these are not academic questions. In several member states, the fiscal position is far from sound. Table 8 (opposite) shows various measures of debt and deficit for each of the member states. The crucial columns are on the far right – "sustainability gap". The countries with minus signs have sustainable deficits, but the countries with plus signs do not. If the real interest rate – the interest rate minus inflation – is 4 per cent, then four countries fail to meet the test: Spain,

Portugal, Italy and Greece. If the real interest rate is 5 per cent, Belgium and the Netherlands join them. We can show this material in graphical form in Figure 8 (page 84).

Those countries in the north-eastern corner of the graph – Greece, Portugal and Italy – are in most trouble.

Table 8 Debt sustainability conditions in the Community

	Debt ratio[1] (1989)	Current surplus[1] (1989)	Primary surplus[1] (1989)	Growth rate (assumed)	Required primary surplus		Sustainability gap	
					r=4%	r=5%	r=4%	r=5%
Belgium	128,4	−6,3	2,4	3	1,3	2,6	−1,1	0,2
Denmark	63,5	−0,7	4,7	3	0,6	1,3	−4,1	−3,4
Germany	43,0	0,2	1,6	3	0,4	0,9	−1,2	−0,7
Greece	86,2	−17,6	−10,1	3,5	0,4	1,3	10,5	11,4
Spain	43,8	−2,1	−0,9	3,5	0,2	0,7	1,1	1,6
France	35,5	−1,3	0,8	3	0,3	0,7	−0,4	−0,1
Ireland	104,9	−3,1	7,7	3,5	0,5	1,6	−7,2	−6,1
Italy	98,9	−10,2	−2,3	3	1	2	3,3	4,3
Luxembourg	9,0	3,3	1,2	3	0,1	0,2	−1,1	−1
Netherlands	78,4	−5,1	1,1	3	0,8	1,6	−0,3	0,5
Portugal	73,1	−5,0	−3,2	3,5	0,4	1,1	3,6	4,3
United Kingdom	44,3	1,6	4,3	3	0,4	0,9	−3,9	−3,4
EC	58,4	−2,8	1,2	3,2	0,5	1,1	−0,7	−0,1

r = real interest rates which are supposed uniform across Member States
Source: Commission Services

How are these figures calculated? Start with the left hand column of the table, which sets out all the key figures. This column is the debt to GDP (national income) ratio. Its development over time depends on four things. The first is the actual amount of debt: the higher it is, the greater the interest payments on it. The second is the real rate of interest: the higher the rate, the more difficult it is to stabilise the debt ratio. (The real rate is important, rather than the nominal rate, because inflation merely pushes up debt and the national income in line, leaving the ratio unchanged.) The third thing is the growth of national income: the higher the growth rate, the easier it is to keep down the ratio of debt to national income. The fourth is the surplus of tax revenue over public spending. The greater the surplus, the easier it is to

Figure 8   Debt ratios and sustainability gaps in the Community (1989)

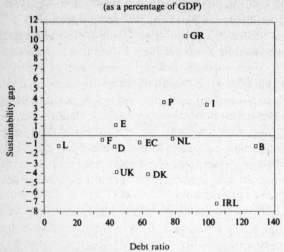

(as a percentage of GDP)

Source: Commission services.

stabilise or reduce the debt-GDP ratio. Since we are stripping out interest payments to make it clear how the debt-GDP ratio reacts to different interest rates, this measure of the surplus excludes interest payments. It is called the "primary surplus".

There are two columns in the table called the "required primary surplus". The more the real interest rate exceeds the growth rate, the higher the primary surplus has to be in order to stabilise the debt-GDP ratio. One column therefore shows what would be necessary for each country if real interest rates are 4 per cent, and one if real rates are 5 per cent. The primary surplus clearly has to be higher if the real interest rate is 5 per cent. The final two columns – showing the sustainability gap – simply compare the actual primary surplus for each country (in column three) with the required primary surplus. This shows, for example, that Greece would have to raise taxes or cut public spending by some 10.5 per cent of national income just to stabilise its debt to GDP ratio even if real rates of interest are at 4 per cent. As a memorandum item, though it is not important in the calculation of sustainability, the table also shows the actual surplus or deficit for each government in the second column. The difference between the actual and the primary surplus is the measure of interest payments.

Clearly, we have to be careful here. A rapidly growing debt to GDP ratio would be of no concern if it occurred in Luxembourg, where debt represents only 9 per cent of national income. But it is fair to assume that debt ratios above 100 per cent of GDP are a real danger signal, not least since it implies, on reasonable assumptions about growth, inflation and the real interest rate, that nearly 10 per cent of national income has to be spent solely on debt service. It must call into question the ability of governments to raise adequate taxation without a revolt. In extremis, high taxes could force migration and the erosion of the tax base.

Can such serious problems be solved? The answer is yes, providing that the political will exists. Figure 9 shows the recent experience of Belgium and Italy. Belgium succeeded, after some initial trials and tribulations in the early eighties, in running a big enough primary surplus to stabilise its debt to GDP ratio. The squiggly line represents a plot of the various primary deficits/ surpluses since 1971. It thus represents what the Belgian government did. The upward sloping line was the target at which the government had to aim in order to stabilise the debt ratio (assuming a 5 per cent real interest rate and 3 per cent growth). It finally hit home in 1989, having moved from a 7 per cent deficit to a 2 per cent surplus, a similar progression to that now required in Greece. As you can see, the Italian experience has not been so happy.

Fiscal discipline ought to be a national matter, but we have seen that a lack of discipline can have an impact on the Community as a whole. Can the Community rely on the financial markets to apply its discipline for it? In theory, the markets might require a higher interest rate from countries whose debt ratios are high and rising in order to compensate for the risk of default. In practice, though, matters are more complex. Would member states really stand by and watch a partner default? Or would their common interest in financial stability provide an overwhelming incentive for a bail-out, rather like the federal government's implicit support for the

Figure 9 Trends in the public debt and primary deficit in Belgium and Italy

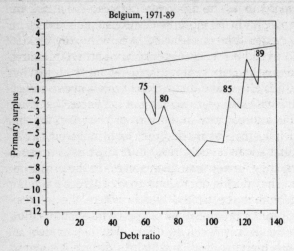

Belgium, 1971-89

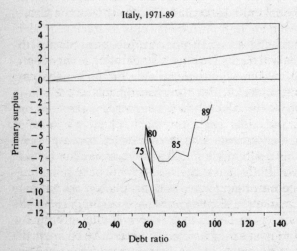

Italy, 1971-89

Source: Commission services

New York bail-out of 1975? Even if they were absolutely firm
that there would be no bail-out, would the markets really
believe them? And would interest rates really reflect the
actual risk or merely a lesser perceived one?

Perhaps even more importantly, financial markets have a very poor record in assessing sovereign risk – the risk of country borrowers. Just before the Mexican debt crisis in August 1982, Argentina was able to borrow money at less than 0.5 per cent above France. Yet within months, Argentina was in default and its debt began to trade at a discount. Why are lenders unable to make distinctions which in retrospect appear so obvious? The best explanation is simply that they set interest rates to contain an element of premium for the risk of all their loans, not merely that loan in particular. If they decide that a loan is more risky than their usual rule of thumb allows, they do not raise interest rates to the prospective borrower. They decide not to lend at all. There is a similar phenomenon within the United States, where the interest rates on states' debts vary by about 0.5 percentage points. But there is even here only weak evidence that higher debt is associated with higher rates. This history does not suggest that the markets would distinguish effectively between Community borrowers.

The commitment of the Euro-fed not to print money to finance deficits will obviously have a moderating influence on national policy makers who contemplate running big deficits, but other constraints on them are clearly relaxed, at least compared with a floating exchange rate system. They can be sure that their own fiscal policy decisions will have very little influence on the common ecu interest rate, because their economy is only a part of the single currency area. This is true to an extent within the European Monetary System now, but it is likely to become more extreme. Secondly, the worry that the financial markets will lose confidence in the currency if the budget is seen to be irresponsible will almost entirely vanish. EMU removes the traditional "balance of payments" and currency crisis constraint, at least in the short term. The risk that countries will respond to the relaxation of these constraints by failing to correct deficits in a timely manner is one reason why mutual co-ordination and surveillance is important.

Another reason for co-ordination of fiscal policy is the mirror image of the above point: national fiscal policies may,

within EMU, have fewer adverse effects on the country concerned, but they also have potentially greater effects on its
partners. First, budget policy will stimulate demand for
imports, and hence boost activity elsewhere. Whether this
leads to a net increase in output depends on whether the
EC-wide interest rate rises as well. Finally, budget policy in
one country will affect the exchange rate of the ecu against
the dollar and the yen, which is also a key variable for other
member states. These increased spill-overs from national
budget policy on to other countries are a *prima facie* argument
for co-ordination.

Let us now look more closely at some of these spill-overs. It
is important to notice that a curiosity of the present arrangements within EMS will come to an end. The curiosity arises
because of Germany's special, central role within the fixed
exchange rate system. As we have seen, the credibility of its
monetary authorities means that the Deutschmark is expected to be the most sound of all the EC currencies, so that
money will tend to be attracted to Frankfurt if the interest
rates elsewhere are not higher. As a result, changes in German interest rates also affect interest rates elsewhere. If the
German government undertakes a fiscal expansion, the Bundesbank is likely to tighten interest rates in order to offset any
inflationary impact. Interest rates then have to rise elsewhere
in the EMS, more than counteracting any indirect boost from
fiscal expansion. In short, a German fiscal expansion is currently a "beggar my neighbour" policy. For exactly opposite
reasons, a fiscal expansion in an EMS country outside Germany has no noticeable effect on interest rates, unless it is so
irresponsible as to call the markets' fundamental confidence
into question. Fiscal expansions outside Germany thus act
like a locomotive for the EC economy.

This lopsidedness ends when all the countries are in EMU,
because the impact of any country's economic weight (which
is what counts in estimating the impact of its fiscal expansion)
would be closely in line with its weight in the monetary
indicators which the Euro-fed would watch. Computer model
simulations on both the IMF Multimod and the Quest models
broadly confirm the above conclusions. For example, a rise in

German government spending worth 2 per cent of national income boosts German GDP by just over 1 per cent in the present German-led EMS, but the boost would be 1.6 per cent in EMU. The effect on other countries would also become less negative. For France, a German fiscal boost now cuts national income by 0.24 per cent because the resulting interest rate rise outweighs the any fiscal stimulus. In EMU, there would be no effect on France, according to Multimod.

If France expands public spending by 2 per cent of national income, the resulting boost is the same within EMS and EMU. There is a positive effect on other countries within EMS, because France is not the lead country for interest rates. Thus German growth is up 0.2 per cent in the first year. However, in EMU, the monetary authorities have to take account of the stimulus in setting interest rates. The result of a fiscal stimulus in France would then be to curb growth by around 0.1 per cent in other countries. Computer model runs using the Quest model come to similar conclusions. In other words, the spill-over effects from a national budget policy move within EMU appear to be small because of the offsetting impact of interest rate and exchange rate changes.

The implications of these findings are very important, because they imply that countries can set their budgets autonomously within EMU without any real fear that they will be adopting policies at odds with their own or the Community interest. There is thus no *a priori* case for strengthening coordination in day-to-day policy making. However, these results crucially hinge on one assumption: that a fiscal expansion normally pushes up the exchange rate. This is meant to occur because interest rates have to rise, and this attracts capital into the currency in a world where capital can flow freely. This does not always happen. At times, fears about the fundamental soundness of a currency can dominate such monetary effects. If a given fiscal expansion actually causes the currency to fall, then the positive effects on growth (and on inflation) will be greater in the short run. This is a considerable area of uncertainty, because there is no reliable computer model of exchange rate movements.

There is thus one foreseeable set of circumstances in which

fiscal policy co-ordination will be crucial within EMU, and that is when there is a serious concern about the Community's combined external deficit, which is in turn troubling the financial markets into depressing the ecu. If the current account deficit reaches serious proportions, it will become the key policy target for the Community. Since higher interest rates have an ambiguous effect on the deficit – they reduce demand and hence imports, but they also raise the ecu and hence price Community producers out of world markets – the correction of this deficit could require fiscal policy changes. But the benefits of fiscal tightening by a national government would benefit the Community as a whole, whereas the home economy would bear all the costs. Without a strong mechanism for co-ordination, the incentive for national governments would be to let other governments do their dirty work. (In economic terms, there would be a free rider problem.)

In the long run, a different set of issues arises. If prices and wages eventually adjust to ensure full employment of capital and labour, the issue might then be whether and how a protracted deficit in a member state might affect its neighbours through higher real interest rates and a higher exchange rate than would otherwise be the case. In other words, should member states be concerned if one of their number unduly appropriates a high share of the EMU's savings? There is no easy answer, but the experience of the eighties with the United States suggests that they would be concerned.

What does all this mean in practice for policy makers within EMU? The answer is that the existing co-ordination and surveillance procedures are probably enough in the short term. The exception would be where there was a problem with the common external account and the currency. This need not have a serious impact on national autonomy, since the objective would be to change the overall policy mix of the Community as a whole. It would still allow member countries to pursue different policies in order to correct the performance of their own economy compared with other members.

We should now turn to three other fiscal issues which arise in EMU. The first is the loss of revenue for some Community governments because they lose the ability to supply cash to their nationals on which they pay no interest – so-called seigniorage revenues. The second is the fall in government spending due to the likely fall in interest rates. The third is whether tax and spending policies in the member states have to become more similar as a result of EMU.

First, seigniorage. This is the ability of the government to finance its spending in part by issuing money. Governments extract seigniorage revenues (also called the inflation tax) by issuing currency to the public or by issuing reserves to the banking system (on which no interest, or below market interest, may be paid). The higher is inflation, the larger are the amounts of cash or reserves which people have to hold, and the greater are the Government's seigniorage revenues. For some member states, as Figure 10 shows, seigniorage revenues are important.

The issue of seigniorage only arises by comparison with a situation in which member states can choose their inflation rates independently, which is arguably not the case in the present stage one of the move towards EMU. Any consideration of the costs therefore has to assume that the alternative to EMU is a free-floating exchange rate, or a very adjustable

Figure 10 Seigniorage revenues in the Community
(As a percentage of GDP, 1988)

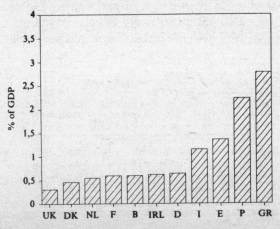

pegged rate. Compared with those benchmarks, what is the gross cost to public finance of reducing inflation? And is there a net cost to the economy as a whole in replacing the inflation tax with explicit taxes?

In most member states, seigniorage revenues are around 0.5 per cent of GDP. But in Portugal, Greece, and, to a lesser extent, Spain and Italy, they are far higher. These countries use more cash and less plastic than other member states, and they also have higher mandatory bank reserve requirements. Because high reserve requirements act like a tax, they put the banking sectors of these countries at a disadvantage compared with the international competition. It is likely, once the Second Banking Directive introduces competition by 1993, that market forces will gradually bring reserve ratios into line. The table shows seigniorage revenues for the four member states most affected, and gives estimates of how much would vanish due to EMU and how much would disappear anyway because of the move towards free competition. These countries will have to find significant amounts of money by raising other forms of taxes. However, they will have low inflation as well as other benefits.

EMU will have other, offsetting implications for public spending. Interest payments on public debt amount to 5 per cent of national income in the Community as a whole. In the most indebted countries like Belgium, Greece, Ireland and Italy, interest is close to 10 per cent of national income or above. Lower inflation will mean lower interest payments, but this will not in itself help the public finances since it will

Table 9 Gross seigniorage revenue effects of monetary union
(Seigniorage revenues as a percentage of GDP)

	1983–84 (1)	1985–87 (2)	1988 (3)	'1993' (4)	'EMU' (5)	Single market effect (6)=(4)−(3)	EMU effect (7)=(5)−(4)
Greece	2,46	2,34	2,75	1,84	0,71	0,91	1,13
Portugal	4,39	2,85	2,23	1,62	0,71	0,61	0,91
Spain	1,93	1,03	1,36	1,20	0,86	0,16	0,34
Italy	2,23	1,21	1,13	0,72	0,51	0,41	0,21

Source: Commission services

also mean that the stock of outstanding debt does not diminish in value as quickly. The real question is whether EMU might lead to a reduction in real interest rates – interest rates after allowing for inflation. Then there would be a real exchequer saving.

Figure 11 Real long-term interest rates and inflation
(Average 1985-89)

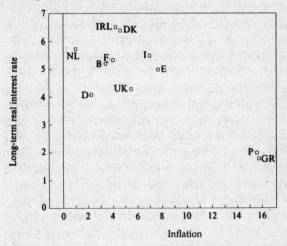

EMU will have some effects on real interest rates, at least in a transitory way. For member states which have high inflation, it is bound to reinforce the credibility of their commitment to price stability. As such, it must also reduce the risk premium which the financial markets extract from high inflation countries. As the graph shows, real interest rates have historically been lowest in Germany, where the anti-inflationary reputation is highest. (The two countries with particularly low real interest rates – Portugal and Greece – are exceptions. They have managed to keep their interest rates down by stopping flows of capital overseas with exchange controls.)

EMU would also eliminate the currency risk of holding assets abroad in a currency which is not that of the home country in which liabilities may well be denominated – for example, for a pension fund. Naturally, such funds will prefer investing in their home currency, and will extract a risk premium for investing outside it. This will also tend to reduce real interest rates.

These benefits will not affect all EMU members equally. Countries with high debt may see their real interest rate on borrowing fall less than others. After all, at present there is a possibility that countries can resort to printing money as a way of servicing debt. If they can no longer do so, it is possible that the risk of default actually rises. However, it is clear that the potential savings can go a long way to offset the losses even in countries with very high seigniorage revenues.

We have so far looked at the gains and losses to public finance which might be expected as a permanent result of EMU. There will also be transitional effects. By speeding up the markets' acceptance that a country now intends to maintain low inflation, there could be considerable gains. The graph below shows how long it took the Netherlands to align its interest rates with German rates despite a commitment to exchange rate stability – there have been only two devaluations of the florin, by 2 per cent each time, in 1979 and 1983 – and ultimately lower inflation than in Germany. Indeed, Dutch interest rates are still marginally higher. If Dutch interest rates had been the same as German ones since 1979, the Netherlands' taxpayers would have saved some 6.6 per cent of national income in debt service. If the interest rate gains were only half as great in EMU, Spain would benefit by some 2.3 per cent of national income and Italy (whose debt is higher) by some 5.4 per cent. These are once-and-for-all gains, against continuing losses from seigniorage. But they provide a useful offset during a transition period.

There is another, final budgetary issue in the move towards EMU. Does it imply that member countries have to bring their tax and spending decisions into line? The answer is that the pressures for minimum standards in taxation will probably mount as the member countries' markets become more integrated. If there is not some agreement on minimum taxes, for example, people and companies will tend to move to areas with lower taxes. Gradually, others will be forced to lower

Figure 12 Long-term interest rate and inflation differences with Germany. The Netherlands and Italy 1974–89

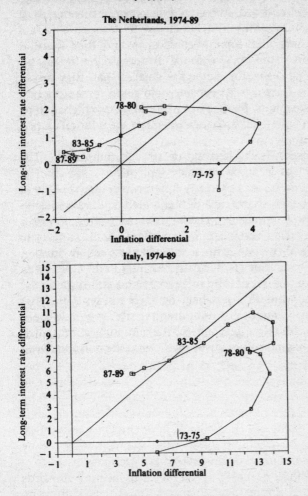

taxes as well until governments are left with a diminished tax base.

These issues, though, already exist in the Community. The broad conclusion of existing research into the field is that there is no need for either income taxes or social security contributions to be harmonised. For VAT and other indirect taxes, which can in principal affect cross-border shopping, the differences in rates merely need to be brought gently into line but not eliminated. In the field of corporate income tax, it will be important within EMU to ensure that taxes are neutral between home and foreign companies and that there is cooperation to stop tax avoidance. In the United States, tax differences between the states are smaller than they are in Europe, but there is still considerable room for autonomy. With one exception, there is not likely to be much change by comparison with fixed exchange rates and the internal market 1992 programme.

The exception is the taxation of income from capital. The introduction of a single currency will mean a sea-change, since there will no longer be any difference in the currency in which bonds or shares are denominated and valued anywhere in the Community. The significance of this is simply that the tax base – the income – can migrate in its entirety to another member state with a more lenient tax regime. A Community solution will clearly be required. One route would be common reporting rules so that tax authorities were made fully aware of assets held by their residents in other parts of the Community. Another possibility would be a common withholding tax, whereby a minimum tax rate was applied to income before it was paid out to the bondholder or shareholder.

5 Coping with change without a currency

Summary

The loss of a separate currency has important implications for the way the economy works. This is essentially because the exchange rate of one currency against another can be influenced by Government policy, and can be used as a buffer to insulate the economy against shocks such as the rise in world oil prices in 1973-74 or 1979-80. It can also be used to help the economy adjust to shocks. This chapter addresses the question of how serious this loss is likely to be, and what other mechanisms would take the place of the national currency and its exchange rate.

The graph on page 98 gives a bird's eye view of the chapter. The right hand part of the graph shows what happens if the shock affects all the Community's economies in the same way: in other words, the shock is common to all. Within this category, there may be some shocks which affect some countries more than others. For example, an oil and gas price rise will disadvantage Germany, France and Italy more than the oil producers within the Community, Britain and the Netherlands. The shock is thus said to be "asymmetric" in its impact, because it affects different countries in different ways. Some shocks, though, could affect all the member states equally (for example, a sharp rise in the price of tropical products such as bananas, sisal and so forth). For this sort of symmetric shock, there is no need for exchange rate changes between the Community countries.

The interesting questions are therefore what happens on the left-hand side of the graph: when an international shock is asymmetric, or when the shock hits one country in particular. This country-specific shock might, for example, be a natural disaster such as an earthquake or it could be a sharp

Figure 13 Schematic overview of Chapter 5

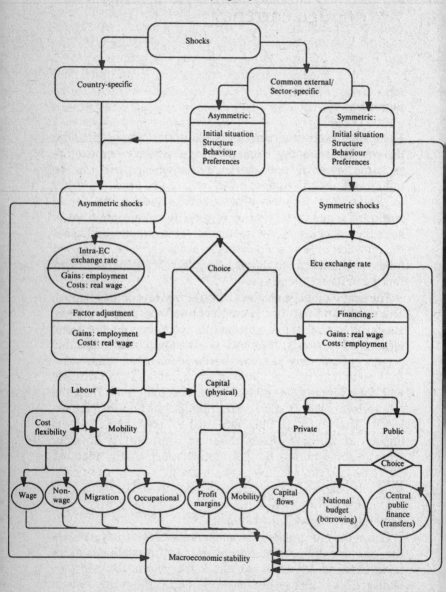

rise in wage increases due to political upheaval. The ability to export might fall. In these circumstances, exchange rates could at present be used to cushion the impact. A devaluation would help business to regain competitiveness despite the shock.

In EMU, this possibility no longer exists. Capital and labour may become unemployed unless they adjust to the new circumstances by reducing their prices or by moving out of the area, or unless the adjustment can be postponed by attracting new capital to fund the new gap between exports and imports. Such financing could be private or public, and public financing could be provided by national governments or the Community.

The conclusions of the chapter are that the fixing of exchange rates – the abolition of national currencies – represents only a very limited loss for the following reasons:

1 The Community would still be able to change its exchange rate vis-à-vis the rest of the world.

2 For the original members of the exchange rate mechanism of the EMS, there has been no serious realignment since 1987. Many of the costs of this fixity have been paid already, although the benefits from EMU have still to be won.

3 Wages and prices do not change in the short run, even in response to a shock. Thus a devaluation of the currency can lead to a real gain in competitiveness (a fall in the real exchange rate, after allowing for inflation differences) for a time. This can limit the effect of any shock on output, but it will also increase the price of imports. This will boost average prices, and is likely to increase inflation. The gain to price competitiveness is thus eroded. In the longer term, exchange rates change in line with differences in inflation without having a lasting impact on price competitiveness.

4 Changes in price competitiveness are still possible through movements in prices within EMU, as the examples of existing federations and the experience of the EMS shows.

5 Taking long-run trends, differences in price competitiveness do not explain differences in growth, since there are many other factors involved.

6 The 1992 programme and the growing interdependence of the Community economies makes shocks which affect only one country much less likely. The growth of trade within the Community is not due to different countries specialising in making entirely different types of products, the demand or supply of which could suddenly collapse. Instead, it is due to finer specialisations in the supply of similar products. In fact, product differentiation is more important than product specialisation.

7 The increased competition in the single European market will ensure that profit margins bear part of the burden of adjustment, leaving less to be borne by labour.

8 Wages are likely to be more responsive to market conditions in a credible EMU, although this will need encouragement. To some extent, there are already signs of greater wage responsiveness within EMS.

9 Additional financing will also ease adjustment and help to cushion shocks, performing a role similar to devaluation but without the inflationary implications. EMU removes one of the traditional constraints on an expanding economy, namely a growing trade gap as imports outpaced exports. Any such deficit becomes easier to finance because investors are no longer inhibited by the prospect of currency devaluation. Budgetary policy can also cushion or aid adjustment.

10 Overall, EMU will probably make the economy as a whole more stable and less prone to inflationary or recessionary lurches. In the past, the fall of the dollar has tended to lead to a sharper rise in the Deutschmark than in other European currencies, thus imposing strains on the EMS. This type of exchange rate shock would disappear, as would beggar-my-neighbour exchange rate policies within Europe. Combined with the greater wage and price discipline which could be expected to flow from EMU will also tend to offset the costs of

shocks affecting different parts of the monetary union.

By comparison with a regime of floating exchange rates, EMU will clearly reduce the variability of output and inflation. Compared with EMS, there will be a smaller gain. But variability should also decrease because the new central bank – the Euro-fed – will be charged with examining the stabilisation of the Community economy as a whole. At present, the Bundesbank runs the key currency within the EMS, and it is statutorily charged only with maintaining low inflation in Germany. However, stability also depends on national policies and the behaviour of people and firms, particularly output stability.

*

The usual starting point for any discussion of the role of exchange rates is the idea that it can help to correct a country's trade imbalance. For example, there might be a sudden change in a country's ability to pay its way in world markets which leads to a large deficit. Imports might exceed exports because it has suddenly lost price competitiveness due to an increase in costs at home. Alternatively, a country might be affected by a change in tastes so that the demand for its exports falls. Classically, a devaluation of the exchange rate would help the economy adjust to these changed circumstances. It would reduce the value of the currency compared with its competitors, and hence make its exports cheaper when priced in foreign currencies. Imports would also become more expensive when priced in the home currency.

It is crucial to note that this mechanism is only useful if it effectively reduces the prices of goods in the devaluing country. In other words, it depends on the proposition that a currency can be devalued without raising domestic wages and prices to the same extent. A change in the actual (or nominal) exchange rate must lead to a change in real exchange rate, after allowing for price changes. A change in the exchange rate – the nominal one – is only useful if prices and wages do not respond immediately. Then a nominal exchange rate change does indeed cause a real exchange rate change.

This is the case in the short run. A devaluation has the benefit of bringing forward any required fall in the real exchange rate so that it can begin its work instantly. The fall in the real exchange rate will normally start to improve the trade balance quite quickly. After a while, though, the rise in import prices affects consumer prices. These price increases feed through into wage increases, which again feed through into domestic price increases. The initial fall in the real exchange rate is now undone as prices rise more rapidly and hence push up the real exchange rate. Eventually, there may be no fall in the real exchange rate at all. If inflation is on a permanently higher path, there may even be a rise for a period.

It is incontrovertible that nominal exchange rate changes lead to real exchange rate changes in the short run: over a three-month period, there is no difference between the two. But this does not imply any link in the long run. Moreover, the link between nominal and real changes is likely to be less strong for the Community countries precisely because they import so much, and the effect of import price rises on domestic inflation is therefore greater than it would be for larger and more self-reliant economies such as the United States or Japan. (The imports of the United States, for example, are worth a mere 12 per cent of its production. But in France imports are worth 21 per cent of production and in Britain 27 per cent.) Formal statistical tests of the link between nominal and real exchange rates for the Community countries between 1980 and 1989 were reported in the Commission's *One market, one money*, and showed that nominal and real changes did not move together for more than four to six quarters.

Another way of testing the same proposition is to look at the results of simulations on the Commission's Quest computer model. The simulations supposed that there was a sharp 5 per cent cut in a country's exports (perhaps due to change in fashion or taste) which has to be made up somehow either by cutting imports or increasing other exports. It then compared the process of adjustment with a devaluation of 7.25 per cent and without one. With a devaluation, the loss of output was 1 per cent compared with a little more than 1.5 per cent without one, while inflation rose by 1 per cent compared with a fall otherwise. In sum, the degree of initial output loss is certainly smaller if there is a devaluation, but the loss goes on for longer before the economy resumes its normal level of output, and it also has a higher inflation rate throughout the period and beyond.

We have now seen how a devaluation can help to correct a trade imbalance, at some cost in terms of inflation. We should now look at the origins and nature of the shocks which could cause the need for such correction. In a perfectly ordered world in which countries had identical economic structures and identical behaviour, real exchange rates would not have to change much if at all. Real exchange rate changes become necessary when the economic system becomes lopsided because some countries are affected by changes and others are not: when shocks or changes in the economic system are said to be asymmetrical.

Clearly, the increase in United States' interest rates which provoked the 1981-82 recession affected all the Community countries equally. A change in Europe's currencies against the dollar might have helped, but there was no case for a change in one European currency against another. The oil price rises of 1973-74 and 1979-80 were different. They disadvantaged oil importers like Germany, France and Italy more than oil and gas exporters like Britain and the Netherlands. Such shocks can arise because of union militancy in one country, or because of a change in the taste for its goods, or because of the impact of bad policy, or perhaps because of a natural disaster like an earthquake. It is also important to note that an apparently common shock can in fact have a bigger impact on some countries compared with others because of the way they react. The more flexible their wages and prices, the less will be the effect on output.

In this context, a crucial question concerns the nature of the EC economies. If the integration of their markets means that they increasingly specialise in different products, then the possibility of shocks which affect only one or two countries in EMU could be very great. If the Italians produced all the shoes, and the Germans all the cars, and the French all the cheese, then there could be serious problems if the demand for one or other product line collapsed. In reality, though, the elementary economic textbooks give a misleading impression of the complexity of the world.

The integration of product markets in the Community has not led to product specialisation but to specialisation within particular industries. In other words, components for a finished product may come from several Community countries. Many Community countries' companies may have a market niche in a particular industry. A recent study by the Commission finds that, except for Portugal and Greece, the share of intraindustry trade – trade between the same industry – in the total trade going on between Community countries varied between 57 per cent and 83 per cent in 1987 (Portugal and Greece have less integrated industrial structures). This implies that a shock which affects one industry is likely to affect most Community countries fairly evenly.

Moreover, a consequence of the 1992 programme is that such integration will gather pace. Integration within an industry typically involves economies of scale, which tends to be held up by barriers to trade. As the barriers come down, integration within the same industry across national frontiers is bound to increase. As a result, shocks will become still less asymmetrical in their impact.

Nevertheless, there will continue to be some asymmetrical shocks, but they should not be exaggerated. The most frequently cited example of a different industrial structure is the presence of oil and gas production. Table 10 shows the effect on average prices throughout each of several member states of a 10 per cent rise in world oil prices, using the data from 1980 when the proportionate size of the oil and gas sectors in Britain and the Netherlands was even larger than it is today. The result, after taking into account the increase in prices of imports from other countries, is to raise domestic prices in Britain and the Netherlands by 1.7 to 1.9 per cent compared with a rise in other countries of 1.3 to 1.4 per cent. This difference is probably the maximum that could be expected within an EMU because the difference in industrial structure could not be greater, because the sector is important, and because the change in world prices can be large.

Table 10 Effects of economic structure on domestic prices after an increase of 10 per cent in oil prices

	With price linkages[1]	Without price linkages
Germany	1,3	1,2
France	1,4	1,3
Italy	1,3	1,2
Netherlands	1,9	1,7
United Kingdom	1,7	1,6

[1] Price linkages – or knock-on effects – among the five countries.
Source: Giavazzi and Giovannini (1987)

What, though, if some countries simply prove more efficient at handling shocks than others? Differences of behaviour could turn a shock common to each economy into a much more serious crisis in one economy than in a more flexible, entrepreneurial one. This difference in behaviour is particularly important in the labour market, because of its central role in determining inflation, price competitiveness and unemployment.

The flexibility of real labour costs depends on two factors. The first is the responsiveness of wages to prices. The smaller the response of wage increases to price increases, the smaller the effect of any wage-price spiral. This in turn implies that an inflationary shock will become less entrenched than in economies where wages respond rapidly to price rises. The second factor is the responsiveness of wages – the price of labour – to unemployment, the symptom that demand and supply are out of balance. If wages slow down very quickly in response to a rise in unemployment, any demand-reducing measures the government takes in order to curb inflation will have to be less severe than in less fortunate economies.

These two measures of rigidity have been combined into one index by work at the Commission, which is shown in Figure 14 on page 106. On this basis, wages are less responsive in the Community than they are in Japan or the United States, but there are nevertheless considerable differences between the main Community countries.

Another way of gauging the responsiveness of different

Figure 14 Real wage rigidity

Real wage rigidity

economies to shocks is by looking at what the computer models suggest. Here, though, we are compelled to admit that economic science comes up with more questions than answers. The Commission looked at four different countries represented in each case by four big computer models with international linkages. The snag? The disparity between the model results for each country was double the disparity between countries.

So far, we have looked at some reasons why countries might want to engineer a change in their real exchange rate, but a further possible reason is that they want to embark on a high growth strategy over a prolonged period. The faster growing country would import more than its slower growing neighbours. If it were not able to expand its world market share due to quality and technology improvements, it would be forced to resort to a regular fall in its real exchange rate – either a fall in the value of its currency, a smaller rise in its prices than those overseas, or a mixture of both – in order to maintain a balance on its trade accounts. This argument is obviously particularly important for countries like Greece, Portugal and Spain which are still catching up.

The argument is, though, wrong. We have already seen

that nominal exchange rates do not determine real exchange rates except in the short term. Trend changes are by definition long-run changes, and must therefore be brought about by changes in prices rather than exchange rates. The exception is countries undergoing serious structural adjustment or economic reform – such as those in Eastern Europe. But the Community countries are not in that position.

The argument in favour of a long-term decline in the real exchange rate is also wrong because the historical evidence in the Community suggests a very weak relationship between high growth and a falling real exchange rate, as Figure 15 shows. Indeed, the relationship fails to pass basic tests of statistical significance. Outside Europe, the notion appears perverse. Japan coupled faster growth than its trading partners with a steady rise in the real exchange rate during the

Figure 15 Real depreciation and growth 1973-88

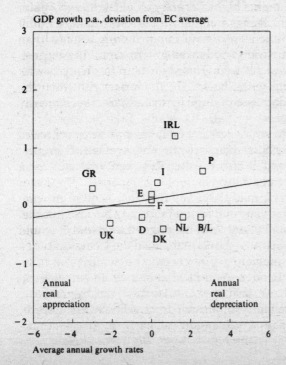

GDP growth p.a., deviation from EC average

Average annual growth rates

sixties and seventies. Other factors – education, training, quality, delivery, management expertise, incentives, research and development, labour relations – are far more important to growth than a trend fall in the real exchange rate.

In the absence of exchange rate changes, an adverse shock to a national economy can be handled in only two other ways. Either prices and wages have to decrease in order to price capital and labour back into full employment, or capital and labour have to migrate towards another region or country. Capital will bear its part of the adjustment through lower prices and profits. Plant and machinery can also be moved, but migration usually applies to labour. The more effective these adjustment processes are, the less transitory unemployment will occur as a result of some economic shock.

The idea that a monetary union would stop price changes in one part of the union compared with another is quite wrong. In existing federal states, the inflation rate can be a few percentage points higher in one part of the country than another. In Canada, for example, the average difference in the inflation rate of eight cities compared with Toronto over the period from 1980 to 1987 was 1.6 per cent. The biggest difference was 2.2 per cent. This short-term flexibility can be useful in dealing with shocks. (In the longer run, though, price inflation does not diverge by more than a fraction of a percentage point across states or regions. Take the experience of the Irish punt, which was linked to the British pound until it joined the EMS in March 1979. The average difference between Irish and British inflation between 1950 and 1979 was less than 0.4 per cent.)

Some of the evidence about pay flexibility is quite encouraging. For example, a comparison of the pay flexibility of the different German Länder with the original six member countries of the Community shows that pay in the Community six responds more rapidly to differences in unemployment than it does in the Länder. Non-ERM countries lie somewhere between the two, so that they are also more flexible than the Germans. Moreover, the flexibility of relative unit labour costs in Germany is weakening while it improves in the Community.

It is also possible that a move to EMU will improve the responsiveness of pay. Because the Euro-fed would be committed to price stability and independent of political pressures, it is likely to carry far more credibility than many of the Community's national governments when it promises low inflation. As a result, it is likely to have a greater influence on pay bargainers. Economic union will also make labour markets more flexible because it will increase the competitive pressures on companies. As a result, a given pay rise may result in more unemployment than would be the case if the markets remained unintegrated and competition was less fierce. Against this, there may also be a tendency within EMU to look at the pay rises and the pay levels of other workers in the Community, while disregarding the differences in productivity. If this becomes a Community-wide "wage norm", regardless of performance, there could be serious unemployment in poorer and less successful regions.

Let us now turn to regional mobility, the other principal mechanism by which a regional shock can be absorbed if wages and prices do not respond. Unemployed workers could migrate to another region, add to its labour force, increase its income and demand and gradually undo the effects of the shock on the Community economy as a whole. However, large-scale labour mobility in the Community is neither feasible nor desirable simply because of language barriers and the human upheaval which is involved. It is also a slow-acting means of adjustment, because emigrants remove both a source of demand and a potential skill from the depressed region which can in turn make it less attractive.

Table 11 shows that regional migration in the Community was running at only a quarter of the level of the United States during the first half of the eighties, which was in turn only half of what it was in the seventies. This lower level of migration tends to be associated with larger disparities of unemployment in the Community than in the United States: the differences in regional unemployment rates comparing nine regions in the US with the Community (excluding Greece, Portugal and Spain) were more than a half greater in the EC. However, the gaps within the EC were only slightly greater than those in the German Länder. This suggests that the lack of mobility and hence equalisation of unemployment rates may have as much to do with a cultural reluctance to move from historical communities and high social security payments as linguistic barriers.

Table 11 Regional net migration in the EC, USA and Sweden
(Average rates p.a., percent of population)

	1970–79	1980–85
EC (64 regions)	0,4	0,2 (1980–85)
USA (50 states + DC)	0,8	0,7 (1980–85)
Sweden (24 countries)	—	0,4 (1985)

Note: Numbers represent total net migration movements across regional boundaries, and thus include movements to or from regions from other Member States and third countries as well as movements between regions within a country. The figure shown for each country is the average of the absolute values of the net migration balance for its regions.

So far in this chapter, we have been looking at the potential costs to countries of losing their currencies as an adjustment mechanism. The extent of this loss depends on the existence of shocks which differentiate between countries, and on slowly reacting wages and prices, without which a devaluation would have little effect on competitiveness. However, there are offsets to these losses. Floating exchange rates have tended to change unexpectedly regardless of policy or the fundamentals. This has been a considerable source of instability in itself, but it will disappear within EMU at least as far as changes against other Community currencies are concerned. EMU would also eliminate, within Europe, the risk of beggar my neighbour exchange rate policies – whether they are competitive devaluations to secure higher growth, or covert revaluations to export inflation and reduce import price rises. (Clearly, these gains are less important to those already in the narrow bands of the EMS.)

Reaching an overall assessment of whether the economy would be more or less stable in EMU is a herculean task. In the real economic world, we cannot conduct laboratory tests. The nearest thing to such a test, just changing one element such as an exchange rate regime but keeping everything else the same, is by using a computer model of the Community economies to simulate what might happen. However, as we have seen, models are far from being uncontroversial, and their results must be taken as indicative rather than conclusive. The Commission has used the IMF's Multimod computer model to see how the Community economies would react in the face of the observed shocks (such as oil price rises, exchange rate and interest rate changes, commodity price changes and so on) which took place between 1979 and 1988. A series of model simulations was conducted, using the same shocks but setting the model to resemble each different exchange rate regime: floating rates, the early EMS, the harder evolving EMS, fixed exchange rates in EMU and a single currency. In each case, policy makers were notionally given the task of using interest rates to keep output and inflation as close as possible to what would have happened without the shocks. The idea was then to see how output and inflation varied with each regime.

The results are most easily summarised in Figure 16 (page 112), which takes as its baseline the effects of a floating exchange rate system. In other words, the variability of output and inflation observed with floating rates is called 100. If output or inflation becomes more variable under other regimes, it moves up (inflation) or to the right (output). The early EMS is thus seen to be an improvement for inflation, but to result in more variations in output. Multimod says that EMU would reduce the variability of output by some 20 per cent, and reduce the variability of inflation by more than a quarter. In other words, EMU will tend to be more stable macroeconomically than any other exchange rate regime.

So far in this chapter, we have looked at the sort of shocks which an economy has to face, and at how it will fare in EMU compared with a situation where it has its own currency. We have also looked solely at monetary policy: the movement of interest rates and exchange rates (if allowed). However, other means of adjusting to shocks are also available. We now turn to the roles of external financing, budgetary policy and the Community's central financing.

Figure 16 Macroeconomic stability of EMU

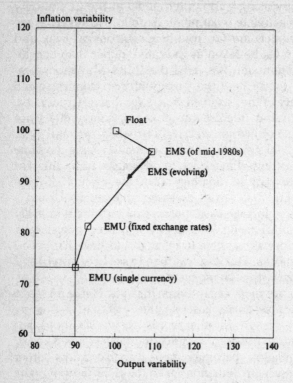

With a single currency, an important constraint on member states disappears. They no longer need to keep a broad balance on the current account of their balance of payments – the balance between exports of goods and services and imports of goods and services, including interest, profits and dividends. While a country has a separate currency, the current account is an indicator of the need for overseas financing. If the deficit of imports over exports becomes very large, there is a corresponding need for foreigners to lend money or buy assets. If at any point, they should decide that their portfolios are sated with such assets, they will demand a sharp rise in the expected return on the country's assets when priced in their own currency. This can only happen if interest rates rise sharply, or if the currency falls sharply, or both. The result would either be much slower growth and perhaps recession, or a rise in inflation. Most governments have thus been careful to restrain the growth of their economies so that imports remain broadly in line with exports. Hence the name "current account constraint" or "external constraint".

Some people have argued that this constraint is rarely operative today, because of the availability of free capital flows to finance deficits. However, that proposition is still controversial. Countries with large deficits – notably Britain and the United States – have had to keep interest rates high or allow their currencies to fall in order to attract foreign funds. Within EMU, there is no such short-term constraint. In the long run, of course, countries may still find foreigners unwilling to buy assets or lend money, but the removal of the risk of devaluation which is inherent in a separate currency means that the concerns are likely to be for solvency, and they will raise their heads at a much later stage. If capital flows were not currently inhibited by exchange rate risk, it would be unlikely that there would be such a close relationship between national savings and investment. In some countries, savings would exceed domestic investment and there would be a capital outflow. In others, domestic investment would exceed savings and there would be a capital inflow. In fact, net capital flows as a proportion of national income are much smaller than they were before the First World War, when the Gold Standard gave investors the impression that that exchange rates were fixed for all time, as we saw in Chapter 3.

The present size of capital flows is also a good deal smaller than it is between regions in existing monetary unions. Among Community members, current account positions over the eighties have ranged from a surplus of 5.8 per cent of national income for Germany to deficits of 4.1 per cent for Britain and 3.4 per cent for Greece. By contrast, Luxembourg, which forms a monetary union with Belgium, had a surplus of 14.9 per cent of national income. The estimates of regional accounts in the MacDougall report give a number of examples of regional current account imbalances of more than 10 per cent of income. Capital flows have probably already increased as a result of the European Monetary System, but

EMU would probably shift flows into a different league.

How useful is the removal of the external constraint? There are two ways in which its absence can substitute for the lost exchange rate within EMU. The first case is where there is a temporary fall in demand for a country's exports, causing a decrease in income and consumption at home. Within EMU, devaluation is not an option. But the same level of consumption could be maintained by, for example, tax remissions. This would cause a further deterioration in the current account, but the shock would be absorbed by means of extra borrowing abroad. In this case, capital flows allow the adjustment to be more gradual than it would otherwise be, and to take place without any rise in inflation, which would be a consequence of devaluation.

The second case is where a country expects a future rise in productivity, but cannot generate the savings at home to fund its investment. A fall in the real exchange rate could encourage exports and discourage imports in order to generate a big enough surplus to finance the investment. Alternatively, it might be easier to finance a deficit (and the investment) abroad because of the elimination of exchange rate risk. For countries like Greece and Portugal, this could be a great boon since perceived macroeconomic risks are often the main obstacle to inwards investment. EMU will thus enable capital to flow to where its returns will be greatest. Free capital flows and EMU will be at least a partial compensation for the loss of devaluation as a policy option.

There are implications for budgetary policy too. After all, tax and spending decisions are a very direct way of influencing the current account of the balance of payments, since they affect domestic demand and imports, without affecting competitiveness. But the virtual disappearance of the current account as a constraint also means that budgetary policy – tax and spending policy – can have a smaller role. It may be of some use in smoothing temporary shocks to the economy, but permanent shocks require price and wage adjustments and should not be delayed by budgetary policy. As we saw earlier in the chapter, budgetary policy also becomes more effective in a world of fixed exchange rates than it is under floating exchange rates. If national governments want to have a target for the current account, budgetary policy will be a more effective instrument for them to attain it.

The final policy instrument which can help adjustment within EMU is central public finance. In existing federations, as Table 12 shows, federal expenditure even excluding social security payments does not fall below 28 per cent of total government spending (in Switzerland). If social security is included, the minimum is 45 per cent (in Canada). This spending includes the provision of a range of public goods – most importantly defence – which is provided broadly equally to different regions. It is thus a more important proportion of income in poorer regions than in rich ones. But public spending also contains an element of social spending which covers part of the personal losses which follow an economic shock. Thus it has a cushioning effect on economic change.

Table 12 Central public finance in five major federations

	Expenditure (net federal spending as % of total consolidated spending)		Revenue (degree of State autonomy)	Grants (% of GDP)
	(a)	(b)		
Switzerland	28	56	79	3,6
USA	54	63	78	2,7
Canada	37	45	56	4,2
Germany	31	67	16	3,4
Australia	40	56	36	7,0

Source: Van Rompuy and Heylen (1986) and Commission services

On the revenue side, the highest level of political authority is generally the most important taxing authority too. Since most tax systems are progressive – they take a higher proportion of income from the better-off – they also contain a built-in element of compensation for economic shocks. A region within a federation which suffers a sharp fall in income will also find itself paying less tax. A third element of redistribution occurs with explicit federal grants, which amount to between 3 per cent of national income in the United States and 7 per cent in Australia.

As a consequence of progressive taxes, flat rate spending, social security payments and grants, the income differentials which would exist between regions of existing federations are reduced by 30 to 40 per cent through the workings of central public finance, according to the Commission's MacDougall Report in 1977. Roughly half of this takes place automatically by virtue of the flat-rate nature of spending and the progressive nature of taxation, and roughly half is explicit regional aid. The effect of these mechanisms is to compensate substantially for temporary falls in regional income. MacDougall estimated that a half to two-thirds of the temporary loss in income may be offset by central finance in unitary states like Britain and France. More recent estimates for the United States suggest that just over a third of any loss is offset. The greater the autonomy of the regions, the less the degree of income equalisation.

The present state of the Community is marked by a high degree of national fiscal autonomy combined with a very low degree of fiscal equalisation. One estimate is that no more than 1 per cent of any income loss in a member country would be compensated by lower taxes paid to the Community. Four arguments suggest that there should be a stronger redistributive role for public finance within EMU.

The first argument arises from considerations of equity and solidarity. If a region finds itself disadvantaged, the collective welfare might suggest some compensation from public finance. A second argument depends on self interest. If the depressed region does not receive compensation, it might consider withdrawing from EMU and reducing the credibility of the whole arrangement and hence the advantages which all draw from it. Others therefore have an interest in ensuring that regional inequities do not grow.

The third argument says that EMU will result in a reduction in public spending unless the centre takes up more responsibilities. Spending will be under pressure simply because governments will find it more difficult to raise tax revenues. They will lose the seigniorage revenue from issuing cash and bank reserves, and they may also be forced to keep taxes down because people will find it easier to migrate to other countries with lower taxes. Fourthly, as markets become much more integrated and imports take a higher proportion of domestic spending, any fiscal expansion will tend to spill over more into other economies, providing governments with less of an incentive to undertake it.

There are several ways in which the role of central finance could be built up. The existing structural funds – the Community's regional and social funds – could expand to support poorer regions. Areas suffering from a particular economic shock could benefit from a Community shock-absorption mechanism which might involve temporary aid, tailing off after several years. In some cases, such as an earthquake or other natural disaster, the need for such a mechanism would be self-evident. In others, it might be more controversial, and would be linked to the sort of conditions on economic policy applied by the International Monetary Fund when it approves programmes of adjustment.

A long-running proposal is that a part of unemployment payments should be funded by the Community, so that there is an automatic element to the way in which public finance stabilises shocks. If unemployment rose in a region, its Community subvention would automatically rise. Such schemes could be revenue-neutral – passing transfers from one region to another on the basis of differences in unemployment rates. They might also take the form of an insurance scheme into which regions paid regularly, and which would pay out only when the need arose.

6 The impact outside Europe

Summary

The main aim of EMU is to improve the Community's economic performance, but it will also have far-reaching implications for the world economy. It will tend to increase the Community's influence in global economic affairs. It may also create a fundamentally different monetary regime for the world economy. Instead of an essentially dollar-based system, we may move towards a system with two or more world currencies. Most of the benefits to Europe of such developments would only arise if there were a single European currency.

The main conclusions of this chapter are as follows:

1 The ecu will become an international competitor to the dollar. Rapid changes, though, are not likely because the dollar's role in trade invoicing and asset holdings is already in decline. In other areas, such as foreign exchange dealing, technical factors favour a single international currency standard, giving the dollar a head start.

2 The growing role of the ecu as a vehicle for international transactions will bring some benefits for the EC. The reduction in transaction costs because more trade with non-EC countries is likely to be denominated in ecus more may save some 0.05 per cent of Community income. The development of ecu trade invoicing would also reduce EC traders' foreign exchange risks. European banks would have bigger opportunities to provide services in their own currency around the world.

3 EMU would also reduce the amount of official gold and foreign currency reserves which the member states needed to

hold, since there would be fewer currencies to manage and fewer flows across the exchanges. The saving might amount to $200 billion or 4 per cent of Community income. The ecu could also become an anchor for currency management in Eastern Europe, rather as the Deutschmark is now in Western Europe. There would also be gains because non-Europeans would want to hold ecus in cash as a means of payment and a store of value, just as they hold the dollar now. This could accumulate to some $35 billion in seigniorage revenue, or some 0.045 per cent of Community income for one year.

4 As the ecu becomes a currency in which trade is denominated, there is also likely to be an increase in the demand for ecu assets. This might be of relatively small proportions, amounting to some 5 per cent of international markets, simply because fund managers have already spread their risk internationally. None the less, this would amount to a large sum of money, and might lead to a temporary rise in the ecu as foreign demand bid it up. The Community would need to be ready to react to any such exchange rate shock by increasing ecu supply.

5 EMU will strengthen the Community's identity in world policy making. Monetary co-ordination should be easier because there would be fewer players, providing that there are no conflicts in the way in which exchange rate policy is shared between the Euro-fed and the Council of Ministers. EMU could be an important contribution towards a more stable world monetary system.

*

The US dollar is the predominant currency in the world monetary system, even though its role has been waning as both Europe and Japan have become major economic players. The emergence of a European currency would accelerate these trends. The ecu would become the major international currency alongside the dollar and the yen.

The likely impact, though, should not be exaggerated. The dominance of the US dollar has already been significantly reduced, with a greater role being played both by the yen and the Deutschmark. In addition, money is a convenience and traders use dollars because they are used to using dollars, not just because the United States is a large part of the world economy and is unlikely to run a rampant inflation. This habit is unlikely to change quickly.

Many of the advantages attributed to the issuer of an international currency also appear, on closer inspection, to be a mirage. The issue of an official reserve currency does not provide any more room for manoeuvre in raising money, since capital markets are open in any case. There may be some saving because Europeans can transact more business in their own currency rather than someone else's. This saves banking commissions, and reduces the risk of being exposed in another currency and seeing it fall. There is also the advantage that foreigners will want to hold the ecu as a means of exchange, rather like the dollar. There is thus some seigniorage revenue to be gained merely from printing banknotes.

But there are also costs involved in having a currency with world status, as both the United States and Britain have historically found. The currency may become liable to shifts in its value not because of any developments within Europe, but because some group of foreigners has decided to buy or sell more of it. Demand and supply can become quite removed from the fundamentals of the economy concerned.

Some idea of the international weight of currencies in trade invoicing is given in Table 13. The first horizontal panel shows the currency breakdown of trade invoicing, while the second panel shows how important each country was in trade. Thus 44.6 per cent of all exports in 1980 were invoiced in dollars, even though only 26 per cent came from the United States. Thus the dollar is much more important than American trade would suggest. The Deutschmark is used broadly in line with German trade, while the other currencies are all used less than their countries' trade shares would imply. The weight of the dollar is disproportionate in imports because it is the currency most frequently used in commodity trade. (The fall in the oil price will account for much of the dollar's apparent fall during the eighties as an import invoicing currency.)

Table 13 Trade invoicing currencies of the six big industrial countries

A: *Currency breakdown of foreign trade invoicing*

	Dollar	Yen	Mark	FF, UKL, LIT	Total
Exports: 1980	44,6	4,6	25,5	25,3	100
1987	41,7	7,5	26,7	24,1	100
Imports: 1980	63,6	1,2	16,7	18,5	100
1987	49,5	2,9	18,3	22,9	100

B: *Shares in total trade of the six countries*

	USA	Japan	Germany	France, UK, Italy	Total
Exports: 1980	26,0	15,3	22,8	35,9	100
1987	21,6	19,9	25,3	33,2	100
Imports: 1980	26,1	15,3	20,4	38,2	100
1987	33,2	12,3	18,7	35,8	100

Source: A. Calculated from Black (1989), B. Eurostat

Figure 17 (page 122) gives an aggregate picture of the role of the major currencies in foreign exchange markets. The left-hand pie chart shows the role of each currency in local trading, in which the home currency is involved on one side of the bargain. The right hand pie chart shows the role of different currencies in non-local currency business. Both types of transactions amount to roughly the same volume of business. The dollar is dominant in both markets, but is absolutely over-whelmingly so in the second. In big deals, transactions via the dollar can be cheaper than between two other currencies. The dollar is also used as a vehicle currency in the market for transactions between banks, so that most interbank transactions use the dollar on one side of the bargain.

What impact will EMU have on this pattern of trading? An important distinction must be drawn between those functions of a vehicle currency which can be shared (between the dollar, yen and ecu) and those which arise from the use of a standard. The second type will shift entirely from dollars to ecu or not shift at all. Trade invoicing is clearly of the first type, and the ecu can expect a larger share. If the share of ecu invoicing were to rise slowly to the EC share of total trade,

Figure 17 Currency breakdown of transactions in foreign exchange markets, 1989

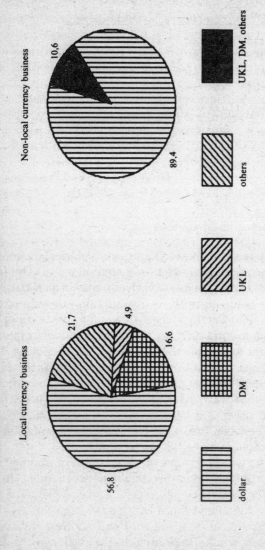

Local currency business refers to all exchange transactions involving the home currency. Non-local currency business refers to transactions among third currencies. In both cases, each transaction is only counted once. For example, the 89,4% share of the dollar in the diagram on the right-hand side means that 89,4% of total transactions involve the dollar on one side. Note that the share of the DM is underestimated due to the non-participation of Germany in the survey, so that the German transactions are only captured to the extent that institutions in these countries conduct operations with parties participating in the survey.

Source : BIS, Survey of foreign exchange market activity, February 1990

some 13 per cent of EC exports and 24 per cent of imports would shift from US dollar invoicing to ecu invoicing.

Pricing of commodities is clearly of the second type: it will shift from dollars to ecus or not at all. This is only likely to occur if the ecu replaces the dollar as the dominant world currency. Since the EC has a similar weight in the world economy to that of the United States, this does not seem likely. In the inter-bank market, any shift to ecus is also likely to be slow. However, the creation of the ecu would eliminate a lot of trading through dollars because of the abolition of so many European currencies. In addition, the European money market would acquire the critical mass necessary to do deals directly with third currencies.

What of the benefits? The reduction in transaction costs could be worth between 0.03 per cent and 0.05 per cent of Community GDP (national income). To some extent, European businesses will be less exposed to currency risk if they do more trade in ecus. Effects of the same kind might occur if oil and commodity prices were denominated in ecus. Europe's bankers would be able to work with their own currency to a greater extent, which would mean fewer risk exposures to insure and better access to their lender of last resort in case of difficulties. There would also be an increase in transaction balances in ecus, which could amount to an additional demand for ecus of $60 billion if the use of the ecu for trade invoicing rose by only 10 per cent of the EC's current transactions.

For governments, EMU will reduce the need for holdings of official gold and foreign currency reserves. Their rationale is intervention in the foreign exchange markets in order to preserve the value of the national currency within its target, or perhaps solely to defend it at times of stress. But the volume of foreign exchange transactions will fall sharply in Europe because all the national currencies will be replaced with one currency. On this basis, EMU should reduce reserves by about the same percentage as the share of foreign exchange transactions within the Community in total forex transactions. This would free some $230 billion in reserves out of a total of $400 billion. Alternatively, the Community could retain the same ratio of reserves to imports as other industrial countries. This would imply a total of $200 billion. The savings would then amount to about 4 per cent of Community income.

The ecu would also be used as an official currency by non-Community countries, particularly perhaps in Eastern Europe and other areas with close economic ties. It is likely that it would be used as an anchor for the increasing number of currencies which are no longer linked to the dollar, but which have varying arrangements such as pegging to their own basket of currencies. The ecu would also be an increasingly useful asset in official reserve portfolios. The dollar's share in countries' reserve portfolios has fallen from nearly 80 per cent in 1976 to 63 per cent in 1988, and the creation of the ecu would surely accelerate the gradual development of a yen-dollar-ecu tripod of world currencies.

There would also be gains to Europe in seigniorage – the revenue from issuing cash which is then bought by the rest of the world in exchange for goods and services merely for the joy of possessing banknotes on which no interest is payable. Estimates of the present dollar holdings outside the US are notoriously unreliable, but the Commission's informed guess, based on research under way at the US Federal Reserve, is that some $100 billion is held overseas in cash. Some of this is likely to switch to ecus. If the switch were broadly in line with the weight of the Community in the world economy, the change could be worth about $35 billion in favour of the ecu. This would be a once-and-for-all adjustment. Thereafter, Europe gains only from the fact that it does not have to pay interest on the money. At 7 per cent interest rates, this on-going seigniorage revenue would be worth only $2.5 billion a year or 0.045 per cent of Community GDP.

So far, we have seen that there would be a shift towards ecus and out of dollars and other currencies. This is composed of an increase in ecus held in private transaction balances at banks to facilitate trade (worth perhaps $60 billion), an increase in cash held overseas ($35 billion), and a reduction in the EC's official reserves ($200 billion). There

could, in addition, be a more general shift in private portfolios of assets towards the ecu. At present, the thinness of
both European and Japanese markets means that international investors are biased towards the US dollar. The
emergence of the ecu would offer private asset holders like
pension funds and life assurance companies a better alternative to the dollar than the existing national European currencies, leading to an upward drift in the demand for ecu assets.
In the short term, this is likely to lead to a higher ecu and
lower ecu interest rates. In the medium term, there may be an
increase in the supply of ecu assets to foreigners if the Community runs a current account deficit.

How big could this portfolio shift be? The problem in coming to any sensible assessment is knowing where to start,
since the figures for international financial flows are far from
perfect. Table 14 overleaf presents the results of the Commission's attempt to draw an overall picture of the gross financial
wealth denominated in foreign currencies. This is not total
financial wealth, but wealth held in foreign currencies.

Two major conclusions emerge from the data. The first is
that the dollar's role is vastly disproportionate to the size of
the US economy: the US currency accounts for 50.3 per cent
of foreign currency denominated assets whereas the US economy accounts for 34.41 per cent of developed country Gross
Domestic Product. Europe, by contrast, accounts for 26.6 per
cent of assets and 33.79 per cent of GDP. The second conclusion is more tentative: there is already a trend for money
managers to diversify their holdings between more currencies. This trend has already benefited Europe at the expense
of the United States.

In this context, EMU would lead to a rise in demand for ecu
assets as the money managers tried to arrange their portfolios
in a way which sensibly reflected the balance of economic
activity, profits and returns. Many financial market participants argue that there is no real alternative to the dollar at
present because European and Japanese markets are still very
inferior. They are inferior in size – fewer companies are
quoted on their stock exchanges – and in liquidity – which
means that it is not always possible to buy or sell because of

Table 14 Size and currency composition of world financial wealth 1988 and 1981

	Billion Dollars	1988 of which in %:				Billion Dollars	1981 of which in %:			
		Dollars	Ecu	Yen	Others		Dollars	Ecu	Yen	Others
World reference portfolio	4 086	50,3	26,6	7,9	15,2	1 652	n.a.	n.a.	n.a.	n.a.
International bonds	1 086	43,3	25,1	12,2	19,4	194	52,6	20,2	6,9	20,3
Other financial securities	1 063	n.a.	n.a.	n.a.	n.a.	641	n.a.	n.a.	n.a.	n.a.
Deposits at foreign banks	964	56,5	28,7	3,6	11,2	572	71,7	16,4	1,6	10,3
Foreign currency deposits of residents	973	65,8	18,7	4,9	10,6	245	68,9	n.a.	n.a.	n.a.
Benchmark data										
OECD GNP (current prices)	14 084	34,41	33,79	20,20	11,58	7 804	34,39	39,30	13,62	12,66
Ratio: share in portfolio/share in GNP		1,59	0,71	0,34	1,2		1,94	0,44	0,21	1,01*

Source: Evaluation by Commission services on the basis of BIS data

the lack of regular turnover. This would be less true with EMU since a single currency would be bound to trigger the unification of European financial markets.

Any estimate of a portfolio shift is bound to be extremely tentative, but a straightforward reweighting in line with the size of international economies could lead to a shift worth 5 to 10 per cent of total financial wealth. The only offsetting effect might be from European fund managers who seek to invest greater amounts overseas in order to maintain the same level of risk, since the replacement of national currencies by the ecu will have removed a source of risk within Europe. Taking account of the trend towards diversification out of dollar assets which already exists, a shift of 5 per cent of total financial wealth – or a little more than $200 billion in 1988 – would seem plausible as an effect of EMU. This is in addition to the $295 billion previously identified as a consequence of reserve savings and so on, making a total flow into the ecu of nearly $500 billion.

The effects of such a shift are bound to be enormous. One consequence is, of course, that far greater numbers of non-European residents will hold European assets. This internationalisation has in the past led to problems, notably for Britain in the inter-war period and thereafter, because the demand and supply of the currency varies with international rather than domestic factors. For this reason, the German authorities have tried to resist the internationalisation of the Deutschmark. Nevertheless, such problems only arise when the international role of a currency is out of line with its weight in the world economy. That would not be the case for the ecu and the Community.

In the short run, the ecu and European financial markets would clearly rise. In the long run, the supply of ecu-denominated assets might rise and the increase in prices would appear to be less pronounced. The basic issue then becomes how the supply of ecu assets would be increased. Clearly, it will not be through the issue of government paper and a build-up in the reserves, since governments will need fewer of them. It must therefore be matched by the private sector. Essentially, Europeans will issue assets to foreigners in exchange for goods and services: Europe will have to run a current account deficit on its balance of payments.

This would not be a source of concern, because it would arise from foreigners' desire to invest in Europe rather than from any weakness in Europe's competitive position. It will be associated with rising European asset values, not the falling ones which would be a warning signal. As such, the capital inflow could help in the non-inflationary financing of the reconstruction of East Germany. Two other sources of supply of ecu assets to foreigners could also come into play. The first might be a higher flow of Community direct investment abroad and the second could be borrowing in ecu by Europeans from the rest of the world.

In principle, this world portfolio shift into ecus should be able to be handled smoothly. But there is always the risk that demand will surge so suddenly that the ecu could soar, causing considerable damage to the tradeable sectors of the Community in the process. Moreover, the increase in demand could well begin ahead of the actual point at which the ecu begins to exist as a separate currency, simply because the markets anticipate such movements and act on them. If so, there will need to be a close co-ordination of exchange rate policies during the transition to a single currency.

So far in this chapter, we have looked at some of the direct implications for financial markets of EMU. There will also be changes for policy makers, notably in the framework for co-operation among the Group of Seven leading industrial countries. EMU may well make it easier to co-ordinate world economic policies. At present, the management of different national economies can be contradictory, rather like two people in the same room, one of whom is turning the heating up, and the other of whom is putting on the air conditioning. Economic research has suggested that the world economy could potentially benefit from between 0.5 per cent and 1.5 per cent of Gross Domestic Product if the Group of Seven could co-ordinate their policies.

EMU might help in three ways. The effects of Community policies would be greater, thus increasing the incentive for co-ordination. (The Community may also have greater bargaining power, increasing its share of potential gains.) EMU is likely to have a major impact since it will in effect reduce the number of monetary policy players from seven to four (US, Japan, EC, and Canada). This should make the exchange of information easier. The co-ordination of policies should also become easier to negotiate and enforce. The only caveat is that fiscal policy would continue to be managed by European national governments, and they would also, through the council of ministers, share responsibility for exchange rate policy. Thus monetary policy would be divided between the Euro-fed and the finance ministers just as it is divided now in Germany and the United States between central bank and government. Nevertheless, the need to present a united front on monetary policy is likely to lead to closer co-ordination on fiscal policy too.

One result of EMU is thus likely to be the genuine development of a tripolar world monetary system based on Europe, the United States and Japan. Is this a good thing? Some scholars have argued that the world monetary system is only ever stable when there is one dominant monetary authority – Britain before the First World War, the United States after the Second – and that periods of transition such as between the wars tend to be marked by turbulence and beggar-my-neighbour policies. However, it is arguable that those strains arose precisely because no one power had assumed responsibility. There is no historical experience in the world economy of genuinely multipolar monetary systems informed by co-operation rather than conflict.

It is equally clear that there is no possibility of a dominant monetary power in the present world economy. Prosperity is spread far more widely than it was after the Second World War, when the United States accounted for two-thirds of all economic activity in the industrial countries. The United States now accounts for just a third. The rise of Japan and the reconstruction of Europe mean it is impossible to envisage the re-establishment of a dollar standard. The theorists who yearn for a single bloc also assume that the world is composed of similar economies with no natural trading or currency zones. The facts of geography and transport costs mean that there are indeed natural economic zones in North America, Europe and the Pacific. Nor does their existence imply that they will conflict rather than co-operate.

The Group of Seven process represents progress by comparison with the period of floating exchange rates after the breakdown of the Bretton Woods system in 1973. Floating rates were characterised by prolonged periods of currency misalignment in Switzerland, Britain and the United States. The move to a more ordered system has helped to reduce the risk of any such chronic misalignments inflicting lasting damage on the tradeable sectors of the economies concerned. If EMU helps a tripolar monetary regime to emerge, as it should, there will be benefits not merely for Europe but the world economy as a whole.

7 The problems of transition

Summary

This chapter looks at the process of arriving at EMU: the transition from a world of national currencies run by national central banks and finance ministers to a European currency run by new institutions. How quickly should the move to EMU happen? The main consideration is the extent to which different costs and benefits arise at different stages, and whether the intermediate stages are indeed stable. Finally, this chapter looks at what degree of convergence of economic performance – of inflation, growth, balance of payments, unemployment and so on – is necessary before exchange rates are fixed. It also looks at how to minimise the costs of reducing inflation.

The main findings of this chapter are:

1 Stage one of the move to EMU – full participation in the narrow bands of the European Monetary System – already yields substantial benefits in terms of exchange rate and price stability. It also implies that countries are paying the main cost of EMU – the loss of the exchange rate as an adjustment mechanism – so long as they rule out any realignment.

2 The full benefits of EMU only arise in the final stage. This is when transaction costs are eliminated and when the Community can play a greater role in world monetary co-operation. Since going beyond stage one would not involve any further costs, so long as countries rule out realignments, this implies that stage two and three bring nothing but benefits.

3 The early payment of costs, and the late reaping of benefits, implies that the transition should be rapid. The main

factor which might set a brake on the speed of transition is lack of convergence on inflation.

4 The transitional stages one and two may not be sustainable. Free capital flows may increasingly force the member states to run similar interest rates if they are to fix their currencies within particular bands. It would be sensible to prepare for a rapid move to a single currency if speculative attacks become serious.

5 The need for convergence of performance in areas other than inflation is debatable. The explosive growth of public debt in some countries will, though, have to be stopped if it is not to undermine the anti-inflationary credentials of EMU.

6 The attainment of low inflation can be made easier by fixing a currency within a credible exchange rate system, as the experience of EMS shows. The most extreme form of this commitment is, of course, monetary union and a single currency. For some of the high inflation countries, the costs of reducing inflation might be cut and the transition period made much shorter if they adopted a single currency as soon as the low inflation countries decided to do so.

The economic costs and benefits of EMU do not only arise in the final move to locked exchange rates: some will occur in stage one and some beyond. Stage one, which started at the beginning of 1990, is when all Community currencies participate in the European Monetary System's fixed exchange rate mechanism within its narrow 2.25 per cent bands, and when any realignment of the target or central rate within the system has to be small enough to ensure that the new bands overlap with the old ones. (In other words, it cannot be more than about 4.5 per cent.) During stage two, the bands within which the currencies are targeted are meant to narrow, and the system of central banks is supposed to be set up but not yet to take responsibility for an independent ecu. Eleven member states (all except Britain) set the beginning of 1994 as the beginning of stage two. In stage three, the Community definitively fixes its exchange rates and, finally, adopts a single currency.

The only alternative to the Delors report's three stages which has been officially proposed is the British government's plan for a "hard ecu". This can be envisaged as an alternative stage two, in which the existing ecu (composed of a basket of community currencies and moving in line with their changes in value) would become a separate common currency managed by a European Monetary Fund. This EMF – rather similar to a European System of Central Banks – would set interest rates on the "hard ecu" in such a way that its target range against other Community currencies within the European Monetary System would never be devalued. If interest rates on the hard ecu and another Community currency were the same, people would prefer the hard ecu because they would know it would never be devalued. Thus its interest rates would effectively be the floor for rates in the system, rather as the German mark rates are now. As such, it would become the centre of the EMS. In time, if people, financial markets and governments so chose, it could replace existing national currencies.

The economic implications of the "hard ecu" may be similar to a fully developed stage one with the German mark at the centre of the system. It is not clear whether its anti-inflationary disciplines would be any greater than those of the present EMS. Any other effects are hard to discern simply because no one can predict whether the "hard ecu" would be widely used as a separate currency. If it took off as a thirteenth currency, there could be some savings in transactions costs, but it is inconceivable that they would of the same magnitude as those from a single currency. Similarly, some exchange rate uncertainty would remain. The "hard ecu" would probably be most attractive in the countries with the highest inflation rates, where it might become an alternative to the domestic currency in wage and price contracts. This transitional phase, before it was adopted as a single currency, could mean considerable uncertainty.

We concentrate, therefore, on the more familiar Delors report proposals. The first question is the extent to which different costs and benefits arise in stage one rather than stage three. For these purposes, stage two does not have significant economic effects and we can ignore it.

The original ERM members, using the narrow bands, have already achieved a considerable degree of price stability. However, there are likely to be some additional benefits during stage three as the Euro-fed builds up its anti-inflationary credibility, not least because there may be an improvement in the relationship between inflation and unemployment. Similarly, exchange rate variability has clearly been reduced in stage one, but will not be eliminated until stage three. Furthermore, no significant reduction in transaction costs is likely until there is a single currency. Conceivably, such exchange costs could be legislated away by imposing a system of "par clearing", whereby banks were compelled to exchange cheques at the fixed rate without a bid-ask spread or commission. However, this would probably only be acceptable to finance houses if exchange rates were irrevocably fixed.

The benefits of the elimination of exchange rate risk may also be brought forward from stage three if businesses genuinely believe that the movement to EMU will not stall. The parallel here is with the 1992 programme. The Commission believed that there would be some short term job losses as a result of the single market programme intensifying competition and leading to greater economies of scale. There would then be a later growth in prosperity as businesses invested to take advantage of wider markets. In fact, there was no short term job loss. Because the 1992 programme gathered real political momentum, businesses began investing ahead of its completion. A similar phenomenon may occur with EMU.

The effects on public finance would be mixed in their timing. The reduction in seigniorage revenue for some countries would begin as soon as their inflation rates fell sharply in stage one. The increasing degree of competition with financial institutions outside the home market would also lead to serious pressures for a cut in required cash reserves held by commercial banks, which is currently a boon for some of the Mediterranean governments. But the offsetting gains to public finance through a reduction in long term interest rates would only arise in stage three. The experience of the Netherlands shows that, even after a long period of stable exchange rates and low inflation, a risk premium can persist.

The main cost of monetary union is the inability to change the nominal exchange rate, because it might be a preferable response to an economic shock affecting one country or region than a slower adjustment of wages and prices. But this cost is largely paid in stage one, because members of the EMS have already committed themselves to infrequent realignments limited in size to the width of the existing bands. Some economists also argue that the nature of wage and price adjustment will begin to change as the Community approaches EMU. With the exchange rate totally fixed, people may begin to realise that they have to react more quickly to an economic shock by changing their prices and wages, because they can no longer rely on the authorities to adjust the exchange rate. Any budget mechanisms developed to help regions undergoing some shock are unlikely to be introduced before stage three.

Finally, the international benefits of EMU are only likely to occur in stage three. The principal benefit is the revenue which the Euro-fed would raise by printing bank notes which foreigners would use as means of exchange, but this international seigniorage revenue cannot occur until there is a readily accepted single currency. Similarly, any gains from better co-ordination of policies in the world economy would await stage three. However, it is possible that money managers could begin to shift into European assets before the introduction of a single currency so long as they firmly anticipated that it would happen.

The broad conclusion from a review of the timing of the various costs and benefits of EMU is thus that the costs are very largely being paid in stage one, providing that governments can be believed when they commit themselves to negligible realignments. However, the benefits which flow from the elimination of transaction costs and of exchange rate uncertainty are only available in stage three. The implication must be that the transition to EMU should be as short as can conveniently be managed.

The discussion so far in this chapter assumes that the Community will be able to proceed, in a timespan of its own choosing, towards EMU. However, several distinguished analysts – notably Mr Tommaso Padoa-Schioppa and Sir Alan Walters – have argued that the sort of arrangements envisaged in stages one and two could be unstable. If the European Monetary System is inherently flawed, then it follows that the only alternative to floating exchange rates is a single currency. We therefore now look at the merits of this argument.

Stages one and two of the Delors plan are essentially a "fixed but adjustable" exchange rate system without any controls on the movement of capital from one currency to another. The freedom of capital poses risks for any fixed rate system. The first is that there will be speculative attacks on particular currencies. One line of argument is that the authorities have only limited foreign currency reserves, whereas speculators can in principle demand to convert unlimited amounts of assets into foreign currency. In extremis, this could force the authorities to abandon their exchange rate target. The trigger for this speculation could be an ill-judged remark by a finance minister, a belief in the markets that the Government was preparing to devalue the exchange rate, or the view that the authorities wanted to avoid any rise in interest rates for either political or public spending reasons. The mere thought that the Government would not raise interest rates can be enough to worry the markets into deserting the currency.

The experience of the smaller countries tends to discount such a view. The Dutch guilder has been pegged to the Deutschmark within a band of only 1 per cent, instead of the EMS limit of 2.25 per cent, since 1983. Despite free capital flows, a high public debt which might create an incentive to keep interest rates low, and continuing public deficits, there have been no speculative attacks on the guilder. The Irish punt's link to sterling until 1979, and the link of the Hong

Kong to the United States dollar, both provide other instances of successful long run stabilisation.

It is arguable, though, that the real potential for speculative attacks comes with the larger currencies such as the French franc and the pound sterling, where financial markets are far deeper and the amounts which could move are far greater. Against that, though, the markets are also becoming used to prolonged periods without ERM realignments. The longer the time without a realignment, the greater the credibility of the system, and the less likely should be any speculative attack against its rates.

Nevertheless, the adoption of a single currency is the only sure way to overcome lingering doubts. Not even an economic and monetary union composed of irrevocably fixed exchange rates is enough, because the markets can always suspect that circumstances might force the rates apart. A good recent example is the case of the Belgian and Luxembourgoeis monetary union. This has now existed for more than fifty years, but the mere rumour that Luxembourg was considering breaking the link by not following Belgium during the last EMS realignment was enough to induce financial markets to differentiate between the two francs. At present, it is still possible to insure against any change in the Belgo-Luxembourgoeis exchange rate, with cover costing some 0.025 per cent. This is clearly a tiny amount, but it does show that the markets are not even prepared to accept this long-standing union as entirely irrevocable. A single currency may be a necessary part of building EMU's credibility.

A second source of instability in the run-up to EMU is currency substitution: even if exchange rates are not expected to change, and interest rates are similar, some currencies may become more attractive than others because they are more widely used in trade within the Community. A shift of money balances from smaller to larger currencies may make it more difficult for national central banks to interpret the stringency of their monetary conditions, leading the country losing deposits to believe that it is tightening and the country gaining them to believe that it is loosening. In reality, the anti-inflationary stance of both countries would be unchanged.

These potential sources of instability during the transition are a further argument for proceeding rapidly to a single currency. The important question is then what conditions need to be met before exchange rates can be locked together? How similar or convergent do national economies have to be before they can safely adopt a single, common currency?

The conventional wisdom is that countries should have very similar inflation rates before they lock their exchange rates together. If they do not, one of them will find its businesses being priced out of the other's and its home market. Not only is it important that price inflation in the markets for goods and services should be similar, but also that wage inflation after allowing for the growth of output per person – unit labour costs growth – should be similar. If it is not, the level of real wage costs to businesses will steadily rise in the country with higher wage inflation, gradually raising unemployment as business profits are squeezed, markets are lost and companies use more machinery to substitute for labour.

In this context, there are three broad groups of Community countries. The first group is composed of the original members of the European Monetary System, all of which are now pegging their currencies to each other using the narrow 2.25 per cent margin each side of the central, target rate. This group – France, Germany, Belgium, Luxembourg, Netherlands, Ireland, Denmark – share inflation rates within 1 percentage point of each other, which is probably within the margin of sampling error for most of the national statistical series. In effect, their differences in inflation are no longer an obstacle to membership of EMU.

In Italy, Spain and Britain, inflation is running between 3 to 5 percentage points higher than the best performance in the Community. However, there is no reason why all of these countries should not be able to participate fully in stage one. In the case of Spain and Britain, they could in time adopt the narrow 2.25 per cent EMS limits. It would be surprising if they were not able to join an EMU within five years, having reduced inflation to levels similar to the first group. The third group is composed of Portugal and Greece. In both cases, even underlying inflation exceeds 10 per cent a year, a rate

which would imply serious job losses if either were to participate in stage one (narrow bands, limited realignments and
so on) unless there were a major stabilisation effort.

A second criterion for convergence is sound public finance.
This we can define, as we did in Chapter 5, in terms of a
stable or falling level of national debt compared with Gross
Domestic Product (the debt-GDP ratio). Once again, there are
three groups in the Community. The first comprises Denmark, Ireland and Britain, where the debt-GDP ratio is falling. France is close to this situation, although the fiscal cost of
the reunification has postponed its achievement in Germany.
Nevertheless, Germany's debt ratio is relatively low and the
investment needs of East Germany are a perfectly legitimate
counterpart to a debt build-up. So Germany and France can
also be included in the first group.

In a second group are Belgium, Spain and Portugal. In
these countries, the public debt-GDP ratio has still not been
stabilised, but the objective is within reach in the near future.
In all cases, it requires an improvement in the primary
balance – a move into surplus – of less than 1 per cent of
national income. This can be achieved, for example, by holding public expenditure growth to 2 per cent for two years in
which the economy grows by 3 per cent. In a third group, the
prospect is not as painless. The trends in budgetary policy in
Greece, Italy and the Netherlands are leading to a rapid
deterioration in the public debt-GDP ratio. They must be put
right urgently, especially in Greece and Italy.

There is a third candidate for convergence in addition to
inflation and the budget deficit, namely the current account
of the balance of payments. However, the case for bringing
external deficits into line is less persuasive, particularly if
they have arisen through private sector borrowing which is
matched by a rise in private sector investment. In a floating or
fixed but adjustable exchange rate system, such deficits might
provoke a speculative attack on the currency. But the present
current account imbalances might be financed without difficulty once capital markets were fully integrated and EMU
had removed any residual risk of exchange rate losses.

Once EMU has taken place, and a single currency is being

used throughout the Community, it will be essential for the wage and price behaviour of the members of the EMU to be similar. To that extent, convergence of inflation is crucial. For the two groups of countries with relatively high inflation, such a change in behaviour cannot be without some costs. These arise, as we saw in Chapter 3, partly because people do not believe the Government when it says it intends to reduce inflation, and partly because wage rises slow down less quickly than price rises. This squeezes profits, and forces companies to retrench their costs, including the number of their employees. Both credibility and wage rigidity affect the speed of the transition to EMU.

One extreme position – the so-called "coronation theory" – is that monetary union should only take place once the economies within the union are similar in all key aspects. At the other extreme, the so-called "monetarist" school (no relation to the view that money supply has a reliable relationship with money demand) holds that the commitment to a fixed exchange rate would force convergence in any case, since it will ensure that goods and services are sold at the same price throughout the fixed currency rate area.

The experience of the EMS suggests a more tentative middle way between the extreme views. The early years of the EMS revealed considerable strains on the system which culminated in a series of realignments. As we have seen, devaluations tended to be of the size necessary to offset any rise in inflation above that of the country's trading partners. So there can be considerable difficulties in making the exchange rate commitment stick if there is no convergence on inflation. This supports the "coronation theory". At the same time, EMS has been a disciplinary device to enforce convergence on inflation. This was particularly true after 1983, when realignments became much less common and EMS arguably helped to establish governments' credibility in the fight against inflation. As a result, it is arguable that the EMS helped to reduce the costs of reducing inflation because wage bargainers responded more rapidly to the slowdown in prices. In recent years, the EMS experience has tended to support the "monetarist school".

All this is saying is that policy makers need to exercise judgement. Without any exchange rate commitment, full convergence might never come about. It might therefore be useful to proceed with stage two and even stage three without full convergence in terms of price stability. The key is the credibility of the authorities. If people and businesses believe that there will be no back-sliding towards separate currencies, devaluations and inflation, then they will tend to amend their behaviour accordingly.

It is impossible to foresee all the circumstances in which a government may have credibility. Clearly, economic history gives examples of currency reforms which were conspicuously successful, notably the German reform of 1948. However, that was a period of considerable political crisis. Other currency reforms have been less successful, and the credibility of the commitment to a low inflation currency may also depend on the starting point.

But it is at least arguable that many of Europe's peripheral countries could join EMU even if they are running what appear to be excessive inflation rates, providing that they undertake a considerable programme of public education and awareness. As long as there is a stable core of countries with a reputation for price stability, some more inflationary countries could leap directly to a single currency. This would be a radical step. It would entail the risk that people would not realise that they had to change their behaviour. But it would also achieve low inflation more rapidly than any other route, and it would unlock the other benefits of EMU far more rapidly.

The balance of costs and benefits from EMU, and the point at which they can be expected, thus implies that the transition to a single currency should be short. The potential danger of instability in the European Monetary System is an additional incentive to move quickly. The main factor limiting a rapid move to EMU is the danger that output and jobs will be lost in high inflation countries if people do not react quickly to the process of lower inflation by moderating their pay rises. These costs are, of course, transitory. The economy will gradually come back to normal levels of output and employment. But the costs may be substantial if the transition to EMU is so rapid that it lacks credibility. EMU will be an entirely new economic environment for people and businesses, who need to have clear signals about the need for a change in wage and price behaviour.

8 The impact on the regions

Summary

So far in this book, we have looked at the overall costs and benefits of Economic and Monetary Union for Europe's national economies. In this chapter, we use economic theory and evidence to assess the regional impact of EMU, particularly on relatively poor regions within the Community. The main conclusions are as follows:

1 There has been concern about the distribution of costs and benefits at every stage of the Community's development: at its creation in the fifties; its northern enlargement in the seventies; the Mediterranean enlargements of the eighties; and now the establishment of the 1992 single market. During the sixties, at the end of the long post-war boom, there was a continued reduction in regional differences of income. In the second half of the seventies and the early eighties, there was a widening gap between the regions. Since then, the gap has remained stable. Overall, then, there has been no long-term trend in regional disparities.

2 The economic literature is dominated by a debate between those who argue that growing economic interdependence aggravates the problems of peripheral regions, and those who argue that integration is more likely to bring the regions together. The early attempts to look at the impact of integration on regional differences concentrated on transport costs and the savings which could be won by producing on a bigger scale, thus spreading overhead costs. Recently, attention has shifted to more deep-seated disadvantages – structural factors – such as a lack of education and training. Business surveys can provide useful clues about regional competitiveness and the reasons for it.

3 Commission studies suggest that rapid economic growth helps to shrink regional differences while recession accentuates the problems of poorer and disadvantaged regions. Convergence between regions occurs more spontaneously among regions and countries which are already relatively mature economically.

4 The Community's regional and social funds – the so-called structural funds – are helping the less favoured regions adapt to the 1992 single market. The financial amounts have been settled up to 1993. EMU will intensify the changes being brought about by the single market and adds to their regional consequences because the exchange rate can be important to economies undergoing deep structural change. The transition thus requires support from Community policies.

5 The key to the successful catching-up of poorer regions lies in making Community and national policies work together effectively. The poorer regions can take advantage of Community initiatives such as the 1992 single market and EMU to take a higher share of expanded activity, particularly if they are accompanied by incentives to relocate and improve the efficiency of local markets for labour and capital.

*

Regions can be defined in geographical, political or economic terms. In many ways, the last definition would be the most useful, since it could bring together areas which were essentially similar and whose problems could therefore be resolved in a similar way. However, the facts of political power mean that the political definition is the one used most commonly within the Community, since a region needs a political centre in order to participate in the EC's bargaining process.

The various stages of economic integration – EMS, 1992 and now EMU – involve the transfer of national rather than regional prerogatives, so that its effects are felt in all the regions of the country concerned. Within the enlarged EC, regional differences are increasingly determined by national boundaries simply because a poor region by, say, Dutch standards is prosperous by Portuguese ones.

There is no simple definition of a regional problem, but it is useful to think of four different elements. The first is that there should be a reasonably well-balanced distribution of population and economic activities through the Community. If a region loses population and activity, it will use its existing infrastructure – its schools, roads and so forth – less intensively. If the services become run down, the remaining population can be demoralised. Social and environmental problems can develop. A second definition of a regional problem is an inadequate level of provision of public goods and services. A third is the inequality of Gross Domestic Product per head compared with other parts of the country or the Community. A fourth is the inequality of personal disposable income per head.

The first objective – a well-balanced distribution of population – is more demanding than any of the others. After all, one of the means of equalising incomes between regions has traditionally been emigration combined with regional subsidies to activity. However, GDP per head is the criterion most often used: it is used, for example, in determining the eligibility for Community regional funds. To satisfy this criterion, the region must have an adequate economic basis to provide its inhabitants with a reasonable standard of living by comparison with the rest of the Community.

There has long been a debate about the effects of free markets and economic integration on regional prosperity. The traditional, neo-classical view holds that economic integration will lead to a faster growth in poorer regions, and hence to a convergence with the prosperity of the better-off areas. This so-called "convergence school" holds that investment will tend to be attracted to those areas where the returns on it are highest, and the returns on investment will be highest in poorer regions because labour costs are lower. The free movement of goods, services and capital should therefore gradually equalise living standards. The subsistence of gaps in regional incomes is, according to neo-classical theory, due to time-lags in the process of market adjustment.

Another group of scholars, one of the leaders of which is Gunnar Myrdal, stresses the mechanisms which cause divergent economic performance. Regional problems might arise in any integrated economic area (such as a customs union like the EC) because the abolition of restrictions on capital movement will increase the attractiveness of highly industrialised centres. New activites will tend to go where the old activities are because of the availability of skilled labour and entrepreneurial experience. Economies of scale are held to reinforce this process of regional inequality, because they provide an additional incentive to expand capacity in the centre which is already developed.

A variation on these themes is the concept of the "growth pole", which is attractive because it offers good infrastructure not merely in a physical sense (such as roads and public transport) but also in business services (accountancy, law, marketing consultancy and so on). A closeness to markets may also be important in cutting transport costs.

The traditional arguments about regional convergence or divergence thus balance two types of effects. The first, which makes for convergence, is that free trade and an integrated marketplace means that areas with relatively low costs can be properly developed. The second, which stresses divergence, points to the advantages of development in an area which is already prosperous, low transport costs in getting goods to market, and the lower costs associated with production in quantity and the ability to spread overheads.

There are two other considerations which ought to be taken into account in trying to assess who might gain and lose from integration. The first is the potential size of the footloose manufacturing sector which is capable of relocating, whether at the centre or the periphery. This puts an upper bound on the extent of any movement. The second is the possibility that economies of scale begin to work in favour of peripheral regions if trade barriers come down entirely. The argument is simply that a modest reduction of trade barriers will bring about relocation to the centre in order to take advantage of economies of scale and the low transport costs due to being close to the market. This implies that barriers – either administrative or perhaps transport costs – remain high enough to outweigh the advantages of the peripheral region's low labour costs. If they come down further, then industry may relocate to the periphery.

The traditional convergence-divergence debate also fails to recognise the complexity of the economic world. Most countries have more than one large centre of economic activity. If a small country's economy integrates with a larger one, and both have established centres, it is quite possible that the centre of the smaller country benefits at the expense of the larger country by capturing more of its hinterland. Small countries are also likely to reap more significant gains from integration simply because the handicap of small markets – and small economies of scale – weighs more heavily on them.

Who gains most from integration is thus impossible to identify on merely theoretical grounds. There are no strong reasons to suspect that either the centre or the periphery will automatically gain from integration. Indeed, there are good theoretical reasons for believing that the overall effect of market integration is likely to differ from one lagging region to another. We must therefore turn to the evidence.

Before we do so, though, we need to enter two caveats. The first is that any global measure of regional problems is plagued by the often arbitary definition of a region, together with the lack of statistics. The second reservation concerns the attribution of cause and effect. We do not know what would have happened to regional disparities if the Community had not existed and, as in all economics, we are not able to conduct laboratory experiments.

The evidence on the change in the gap between the regions is quite encouraging. Overall, the period since the foundation of the European Community has marked the strongest convergence of national income of its members for one hundred and fifty years, which is broadly as far as the available statistics for the European economies will take us. This at least implies that the Community's integration has had no very adverse effects.

Nevertheless, the trend of convergence was interrupted during the period of weak growth during the seventies. One reason why poorer regions are harder hit by a slowdown is that they tend to contain a higher proportion of small and marginally efficient firms which grow more rapidly in booms, and more slowly in recessions. Secondly, poorer regions also tend to receive a higher share of public investment, which is prone to cutbacks during periods of retrenchment. They also receive a higher proportion of new private sector investment, which is very responsive to the business cycle.

As Table 15 shows, there may have been an improvement in the late eighties which is consistent with the overall improvement in the Community economy. Taking the Theil co-efficient, which is merely the ratio of the weakest to the strongest regions' GDP after allowing for their size, regional inequality appears to have stopped growing worse in the late eighties. It is too early to say that a convergent trend has resumed.

Though the gap has closed in the post-war period, it remains considerable. International comparisons show that regional disparities within the Community are greater than in other economically integrated areas. For example, the gap between regional incomes is about twice as great as in the United States. If the criterion is the nature and sophistication of the industry in each region, then there is a clear centre-to-periphery pattern. There is also a slope, running from sophisticated to less so, from the north-east corner of the Community (Germany, Denmark, Netherlands) to the south-west corner (Spain, Portugal). A recent study for the Commission constructed an "index of peripherality" which took account of a relative income and proximity to large markets. Its results are shown in the map, which draws contours which mark those regions above given percentages of the Community average. Beyond the outermost ring is an area which represents some 40 per cent of the Community's surface, a fifth of its population, and only 13 per cent of its Gross Domestic Product.

Tables 17 and 18 (pages 154–5) show some key indicators for poor and rich regions in different federations. It is noticeable that the best-off tenth – the top decile – of Community regions is 2.6 times better off (in terms of GDP per head) than the worst-off tenth. As Table 17 below shows, this compares with a ratio of 1.7 in the United States. What explains the

Table 15 Disparities in GDP per head in EC-12, 1980–88
(Average = 100)

	1980	1981	1982	1983	1984	1985	1986	1987	1988
Average 10 weakest regions	47	46	46	45	45	45	45	45	45
Average 10 strongest regions	145	146	147	149	149	150	151	151	151
Weighted coefficient of variation	26,1	26,5	26,8	27	27,2	27,5	27,9	27,5	27,5

Source: Commission services

Figure 18   How peripheral are Europe's regions?
(Regional peripherality indices, 1983. Contours as percentage of EC 12 average)

> 150 inner central
120–150 outer central
70–120 intermediate
60–70 inner peripheral
< 60 outer peripheral

Table 16 Shares of central, intermediate and peripheral regions, 1983
(EC 12 = 100)

	Number of regions	Area %	Population %	GDP (PPS) %	Employment				Unemployment		
					Total %	Agric. %	Manuf. %	Serv. %	Total %	Young %	Wom. %
Central	44	10,0	31,0	37,9	35,6	11,6	37,9	38,8	31,5	25,8	29,5
inner	25	5,0	21,7	28,2	25,4	6,3	24,7	28,6	21,0	16,6	20,3
outer	19	5,0	9,3	9,7	10,2	5,3	13,2	10,2	10,5	9,2	9,3
Intermediate	62	33,9	35,7	37,0	37,0	31,6	40,0	36,5	29,3	29,4	31,2
Peripheral	60	56,1	33,3	24,5	27,4	56,8	22,1	24,7	39,3	44,8	39,3
inner	19	15,1	13,0	11,6	10,4	12,2	9,2	10,6	16,0	17,7	16,1
outer	41	40,2	20,3	12,9	17,0	44,6	12,9	14,1	23,3	27,2	23,2
EC 12	166	100,0	100,0	100,0	100,0	100,0	100,0	100,0	100,0	100,0	100,0

[1] See map above
Source: Keeble et al. (1988)

much smaller regional differences in the United States and other federations despite its greater geographical spread and its natural diversity? Part of the difference – for example between Canada and the Community – can be explained merely because the regions within Canada are smaller. The smaller the regions being compared, the more likely it is that there will be an above- or below-average area. (This is why the relationship between the top tenth and the bottom tenth is greater in the Community if regions are compared than if countries as a whole are compared.)

However, the principal reasons for the reduction of regional differences in federations are the mobility of people within the country and the automatic financial transfers which operate through a progressive tax system which takes a higher proportion of tax from those with high incomes, and a flat-rate or progressive public expenditure system which distributes spending equally. As we saw in Chapter 5, the Community budget is not large enough to fulfil the same function even if there was a political will for it to do so.

Nevertheless, the Community has been concerned with regional issues ever since its inception. In the late fifties and early sixties, there was considerable concern about the impact of integration on regions which depended particularly on traditional and declining industries like coal and steel. There were some regional safeguards in the Treaty of Rome articles covering agriculture, transport and competition policy, but essentially it was assumed that the dynamic effects of the creation of the Community would benefit the poorer regions as well. The only EC institution specifically charged with regional policy was the European Investment Bank. Most regional policy was left in the hands of national governments.

In 1970, the Werner report on monetary union argued that there had to be measures to help economic change as part of the process of integration. The first enlargement brought in new problem regions, and the 1973 oil price shock precipitated a recession which deepened regional disparities. These events marked a turning point in an acceptance of a Community role in regional or so-called "structural" policies.

The first movement towards a regional policy at Community level was the adoption in 1971 of the principles of co-ordination of regional aid regimes, which aimed to avoid competitive subsidies which could make aid ineffective. In 1975, the European Regional Development Fund was founded, and was greatly expanded at the time of the Mediterranean enlargement. The Guidance section of the European Agricultural Guidance and Guarantee Fund (EAGGF or FEOGA after its French initials) was introduced in the early seventies to help wean labour off the land. The European Social Fund had been part of the Community's policies from the beginning, but was significantly reformed in 1972 and 1977. It also had a regional objective explicitly included.

It must, though, be said that the structural funds are the only part of the Community budget which are explicitly redistributive from the well-off to the worse-off. The bulk of agricultural spending goes in supporting market prices for farmers, and distributing income from food consuming areas (regardless of income) to food producing areas (regardless of income). Moreover, the structural funds represent a fifth of a budget total which at maximum must account for less than 1.2 per cent of Community GDP. The structural funds currently account for less than 0.25 per cent of Community GDP. Evidently, the redistributive effects are negligible by comparison with those of tax and spending systems in existing federations. As we saw in Chapter 6, federal grants alone account for 3 per cent of national income in the United States and 7 per cent in Australia, more than double and treble the Community proportion.

This lack of a strong central finance role for the Community is not necessarily an obstacle to EMU, since it is quite likely that the poorer regions will gain from further integration. It merely represents the relative lack of social solidarity in the Community, at least in its current stage of development, by comparison with existing federations and unitary states.

So far in this chapter, we have discussed the possible effects of EMU on the regions which we might expect from economic theory, and we have looked at the existing policy response from the Community. We now turn to the

Table 17 Gross Domestic Product per head (international comparisons)

	Ratio of top to bottom deciles[1]	Coefficient of variation[2]
EC (60 regions, 1986 data in PPS)[3]	2,6	25,2%
EC (12 Member States)	2,0	17,6%
Germany (11 Länder)	1,6	13,7%
USA (50 states + D. of Columbia, 1986)[4]	1,7	16,1%
Canada (10 provinces + 1 region, 1984)[5]	2,2	20,1%

[1] Deciles defined in terms of population. Averages for top and bottom deciles obtained by linear interpolation. In the EC the regions covering the top decile are: Nord-Ouest, Emilia-Romagna and Lombardia (Italy), Bremen and Hamburg (Germany), Noord-Nederland, Bruxelles and Île de France. The regions covering the bottom decile are: Portugal, Greece, Sur and Centro (Spain) and Ireland

[2] Weighted

[3] *Source:* Eurostat, *Statistical indicators for the reform of the structural Funds*, November 1988

[4] *Source:* US Department of Commerce, *Survey of current business*, May 1980

[5] *Source:* Ministry of Supply and Services, *Canada Year Book 1988*

Table 18 Unemployment rates

	Ratio of top to bottom deciles[1]	Coefficient of variation[2]
EC (60 regions, averages 1986–88)[3]	5,1	46,9%
EC (12 Member States, averages 1986–88)	4,0	37,4%
Germany (11 Länder, averages 1986–88)	12,9	33,0%
USA (50 states + D. of Columbia, averages 1986)[4]	2,3	22,8%
Canada (10 provinces only, averages 1984–86)[5]	2,1	25,6%

[1] Deciles defined in terms of labour force. Averages for deciles obtained by linear interpolation. In the EC the regions covering the bottom (best) decile are: Rheinland-Pfalz, Hessen, Bayern and Baden-Württemburg (Germany) and Luxembourg (Grand Duchy). The regions covering the top (worst) decile are: Sur, Canarias, Este, Noreste, Centro and Madrid (Spain), Campania and Sardegna (Italy) and Northern Ireland (UK)

[2] Weighted

[3] *Source*: Eurostat, *Statistical indicators for the reform of the structural Funds*, November 1988

[4] *Source*: US Department of Commerce and Census Bureau, *Statistical Abstract of the United States 1988*

[5] *Source*: Ministry of Supply and Services, *Canada Year Book 1988*

Table 19 The structural funds and the EC budget, 1970–90

	1970		1975		1980		1985		1990	
	Mecu	%	Mecu	%	Mecu	%	Mecu	%	Mecu	%
Regional			75,3	1,2	1 126,4	7,0	2 495,3	8,8	4 704,5	10,1
Social			157,9	2,5	1 014,2	6,3	2 188,5	7,8	3 321,9	3,1
Agriculture			158,8	2,6	624,7	3,9	852,9	3,0	1 449,0	3,1
Total funds	64,0	1,2	392,0	6,3	2 765,3	17,2	5 536,6	19,6	9 475,4	20,2
Total EC budget	5 448,4	100,0	6 213,6	100,0	16 057,5	100,0	28 223,0	100,0	46 808,7	100,0

Source: European Economy No 42: Court of Auditors' Annual Report, several issues

perception of businesses about regional handicaps and the effect of policy measures. The surveys conducted for the EC Commission are particularly valuable because they give an indication of business confidence, which will in turn determine whether private investment undergoes the sort of surge which accompanies the move towards 1992, with thoroughly beneficent effects on the Community economy. It also gives some indication of regional differences in confidence.

The surveys show that optimistic expectations about the effects of the European single market and the economic part of EMU are widespread in the Community countries, but they are not shared equally in all regions. Table 20 below shows the results of a 1989 survey where businessmen were asked to assess the likely impact of the completion of the internal market on their companies and their host region. This survey was organised by the IFO institute of Munich, and covered some 9,000 companies situation in three types of region: lagging, declining industrial, and prosperous. Fifty-five regions were covered: forty-five problem ones and ten prosperous ones for the purposes of comparison.

The companies in the prosperous regions are more positive about their own and their region's prospects than companies in problem regions. There is less optimism about the prospects for declining regions than there is for lagging ones. These, though, are broad generalisations from the survey evidence. There are number of exceptions to them which suggest that it is not possible to predict the distribution of EMU's benefits between prosperous and poorer regions. For Britain and the Netherlands, firms in declining industrial regions think that the impact of the internal market will be more positive than firms in prosperous regions. In Spain, firms in lagging regions are more optimistic than their counterparts in the two other types of region.

The detail of the survey data suggests that bigger firms are more optimistic than smaller ones, particularly in the lagging regions. Not surprisingly, the greater the concentration of the firm on foreign markets, the more optimistic it tends to be about the single market. Firms producing investment goods and business services are also more optimistic than those producing intermediate goods (components for other products) and consumer goods.

The IFO survey also provides insights into the factors which businesses believe to be responsible for slowing their growth. It thus allows us to reach some assessment of whether these factors are inherently regional – such as geographic distance from the centre of markets – or whether they can be changed – such as the quality of education and training. These are presented in the table below. The answers to the question about exchange rate policy are particularly interesting. They show that in the "control" regions – that is, the prosperous ones used to establish a benchmark against which to measure regional effects – there was a balance of 20 per cent of the sample which thought that exchange rate policy was negative for regional competitiveness. In lagging regions, the answer was almost exactly the same: 21 per cent. However, in declining regions, the negative balance was actually much smaller at 7 per cent. This suggests that the exchange rate does not affect businesses in problem regions more acutely than those elsewhere, which in turn suggests that monetary union might have a relatively neutral impact between regions.

Table 20   Company assessment of factors of regional competitiveness

	Lagging	Declining	Control
National factors			
Exchange rate policy	−21	−7	−20
Income/corporate taxation	−70	−64	−76
Cost of credit	−98	−32	−45
Availability of risk capital	−18	−8	5
General economic growth	44	68	72
Sector's outlook	34	55	46
Wage costs	−42	−53	−79
Indirect labour costs	−79	−99	−120
Labour market regulation	−62	−67	−78
Industrial policy	1	0	10
Legal regulations	−2	−22	−27

	Control	Lagging	Declining
National factors			
Administrative procedures	−38	−36	−31
Other macro factors	−2	−9	−5
Regional factors			
Proximity of customers	57	−51	68
Proximity of suppliers	36	22	45
Business culture	31	10	11
Banks, insurance, lawyers	60	32	52
Advertising and consulting	40	14	24
Servicing machinery	47	9	42
Transport network	66	16	70
Supply and cost of energy	30	−18	18
Communication systems	58	29	74
Waste disposal	−12	−21	−3
Industrial sites	−7	−3	10
Cultural and social facilities	24	−13	16
Leisure facilities	19	−13	21
Social climate	36	17	21
Cost of housing	−16	−18	18
School facilities	38	−3	25
Supply of qualified labour	−25	−18	−29
Supply of unqualified labour	−2	14	15
Proximity of training	37	−15	21
Proximity of higher education	40	7	42
Regional policy incentives	3	1	2
Cooperation of local authorities	−10	−17	0
Local taxes	−41	−32	−57
Other regional factors	6	3	0

Source: IFO (1989)

In order to highlight the differences between the answers from businesses in the poorer regions compared with those in the prosperous regions, the same information is presented in Figure 19 opposite. However, instead of showing the actual balances in each case, the graph shows the difference between the balances in the poorer regions and the prosperous regions. Thus the exchange rate policy line shows that the lagging region was very near zero: i.e. it was close to the prosperous region's answers. The answers for the declining region were less pessimistic than those for the prosperous regions, so that it shows up on the positive side of zero.

Among the regional factors, the physical distance to markets is not perceived as a serious disadvantage in the lagging, and often peripheral, regions. Instead, the lack of certain types of infrastructure such as transport, communications, social facilities and so on is seen as much more important. Geographical disadvantage is thus perceived as being less important than forms of backwardness which can be changed.

Taking basic infrastructure, for example, Greece and Portugal have less than one-tenth and one-fifth of the EC average for kilometres of motorway per square kilometre. The number of telephone lines per thousand inhabitants in the poorer regions of Spain is less than half of the EC figure. In East Germany, it is less than a quarter.

The poorer regions also have a poorly qualified labour force which reflects the poor performance of the countries' education systems. In Greece, total public spending on education amounted to 2.9 per cent of national income in 1986 while the EC average was 4.8 per cent. Spending per pupil in Greece is only 28 per cent of the EC average while in Portugal and Greece it amounts to 40 per cent and 51 per cent respectively. The school-leaving age in the more developed parts of the Community ranges from 15½ in France to 18 in Belgium, whereas in all the five poorest EC countries the limit is earlier. The potential for increasing education and productivity in these countries is therefore very large.

Some have expressed the concern that, if these underlying

Figure 19 Enterprise assessment of factors behind regional competitiveness

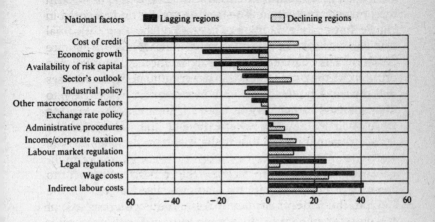

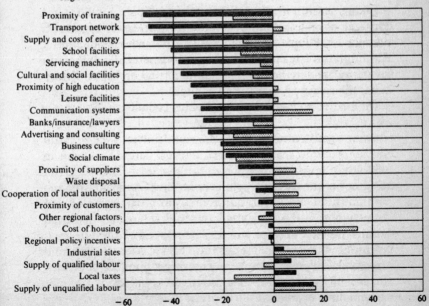

issues are not tackled, one of the ways in which the peripheral regions of the Community coped with EMU would be through a renewal of emigration. The lagging regions and countries of the EC have a long tradition of migration from the south, west and east towards the central member states. Nevertheless, the situation has changed significantly in the last two decades. Although European integration has continued, it has not been accompanied by the large-scale movements of labour which characterised earlier periods. Indeed, Ireland is the only less developed EC country where there is still net emigration, mostly towards Britain where the Irish face no language barrier. The only exception may prove to be emigration from the eastern part of Germany to the western parts, although this too may prove less significant than some had feared.

True, the freedom for the Spanish and Portuguese to look for work anywhere in the Community will only take place from 1993 onwards, and it is possible that migration to the rest of the EC will take place. However, the experience of Italy and Greece is instructive. In neither case was there any large flow of labour when free movement was introduced. Moreover, there is no tradition of migration between Spain and Portugal. This lack of migration compared with earlier times is probably because of the rise in wage levels in the emigrant countries. Although the wage differential may remain large, the absolute level of wages in the poorer countries is much higher. Moreover, the prosperity of the rural areas has improved greatly since the fifties, and they have always been a prime source of any exodus.

Being small economies which are reliant on foreign trade, the increase in economic welfare must largely come from exploiting opportunities in world markets. The industrial structure of the lagging regions is decisive. A recent Commission study analysed the different sectoral strengths of each country within the 1992 single market. It showed that trade within industry sectors was less developed in the European countries with low income per head and was less important in Greece and Portugal than in any other member countries. Spain and Ireland, and in some respects Italy too, are in an intermediate position.

The industrial sectors in the lagging countries could develop in two ways. A first scenario would consist of specialisation in trade of largely finished goods between industries and between industry and consumer. A second scenario would follow the pattern of the more advanced EC countries, with firms developing links with other firms in the same industrial sector. Intraindustry trade would dominate. Neither scenario is necessarily better than the other, and a combination is likely. But intraindustry trade would make the region and the country less susceptible to shocks which might affect sectors on which it was reliant.

On either scenario, foreign investment will play a crucial role. In order to secure inflows of foreign capital, peripheral regions have to provide conditions in which investors can earn an attractive return. The performance so far of the newest EC members – Spain and Portugal – is quite striking. Since 1986, there has been a take-off in their trade with the rest of the Community together with a boom in foreign direct investment. Figure 20 shows both trade and direct investment as a proportion of Spanish and Portuguese national income.

Figure 20 Spain and Portugal – trade and investment flows with the rest of the Community

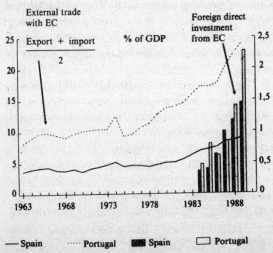

The key question is whether monetary union, coming on top of the integration set off by the 1992 programme and economic union, will have any particular regional effects. The two most important issues for the lagging regions are the abandonment of a currency – of the nominal exchange rate – and the elimination of hidden forms of taxation in the form of seigniorage, analysed in chapters 4 and 5.

Neither issue is particular to low income regions, but both may have particularly intense effects in them. For example, there is evidently a higher risk for a country or region which does relatively little trade within a particular sector or industry of being hit by a shock affecting only those sectors in which it specialises. Perhaps the most obvious example, in the case of the Mediterranean countries, might be some pollution or other scare affecting tourism. Handling this sort of shock is easier if there is a currency available to cushion the process of adjustment.

There is an additional reason why, for at least some of the poorer countries, a separate currency may be particularly useful. In the case of Greece, its economy is a long way from the pattern which would be dictated by the free play of markets – in other words, it is substantially distorted. To a lesser extent, this applies to Portugal. There are relatively few costs for undistorted economies in accepting a single currency with others, particularly if their costs (including real wages) are broadly in line. However, there may be substantial disadvantages in a severely distorted economy giving up a mechanism which can help it to adjust to world markets and their prices. These distortions are already being tested by the impact of the single market programme, which is the equivalent to a whole series of shocks for economies used to substantial degrees of protection.

The issue of abandoning a separate currency does not, of course, arise for many of the Community's lagging regions since they are already a part of a currency area with more prosperous regions. This is the case for both Spain's and Italy's poor regions. It is also, of course, the case for Germany's eastern Länder, formerly in east Germany. Effectively, therefore, we are talking about the three countries which are eligible for support from the Community's structural funds: Greece, Ireland and Portugal. Within this group, Ireland is a special case because it has participated in the European Monetary System since the beginning in 1979. Indeed, it has avoided any devaluation within the ERM since 1986. Given the turnaround in its public finances, this is probably sustainable. Ireland is already relying on changes in relative prices, rather than the exchange rate, in order to allow its economy to adjust to world markets.

The abandonment of a separate currency would thus involve a real sacrifice only for Portugal and Greece, which both follow autonomous exchange rate policies. Portugal has, for more than a decade, operated a regular system of devaluations whereby the currency is reduced in line with the extent to which its inflation exceeds its trading partners. This "crawling peg regime" is reinforced periodically with additional devaluations, although the last was in 1983. Greece has followed a policy of managed floating, which it has used to secure the largest overall devaluation of all Community countries since 1979. Some argue that Greece's very different industrial structure increases the possibility of shocks which would justify devaluations, and that it should avoid early membership of the EMS.

The second issue which particularly concerns the lagging regions in the Mediterranean is the loss of seigniorage revenue, which is bound to increase the public expenditure contraints of the lagging regions while alternative forms of taxation are put in place. It is likely that there would be some increase in central public finance in the Community as a result of EMU, but this too would tend to increase the demands on national public spending. The transfers of the Community's structural funds, which can amount to 3 per cent of GDP in the case of Greece and Portugal, rely on national governments matching the Community contribution. The spending has to be additional to whatever the government would anyway have undertaken – the so-called "additionality" principle.

Monetary union is also likely to have an additional impact on the lagging regions by accelerating changes in their

Table 21 Less favoured regions and Community structural policies for the period 1989-93
(Public expenditure considered in the Community support framework (CSF))

Regions	Total (1)=(2)+(3)	Structural Funds (2)	National finance requirement (3)	Community loans (EIB, ECSC)
In Mecu, 1989 prices				
Greece (entire country)	12 995	7 195	5 802	1 410
Ireland (entire country)	6 126	3 672	2 454	560
Portugal (entire country)	14 026	7 368	6 658	2 805
Spain (70% of the country)	16 507	9 779	6 728	2 206
Italy (Mezzogiorno)	14 062	7 583	6 479	1 475
in % of regional GDP				
Greece (entire country)	5,2	2,9	2,3	
Ireland (entire country)	3,8	2,3	1,5	
Portugal (entire country)	6,6	3,5	3,1	
Spain (70% of the country)	2,0	1,2	0,8	
Italy (Mezzogiorno)	1,5	0,8	0,7	

Table 22 CSF public expenditure – breakdown by main categories in percentages

	Portugal	Spain	Italy	Ireland	Greece
Infrastructure	27,3	53,1	47,3	17,1	31,3
Aids to product investment	17,0	9,9	29,0	26,5	7,0
Agriculture	11,9	14,0	8,3	24,5	13,0
Manpower	28,0	22,7	14,8	31,2	13,7
Regional programmes	15,6	1	1	1	34,5
Others	0,2	0,3	0,6	0,6	0,4
Total	100	100	100	100	100

[1] Included in the other categories

financial systems. At present, the financial systems in the poorer countries are often underdeveloped, and have a particularly close relationship with the monetary authorities because of the need to finance large public sector deficits through seigniorage (in the form of high, mandatory bank cash reserve requirements). Direct controls imposed to regulate credit often crowd the private sector out of the market. EMU will make it easier for foreign banks to compete, and will ease both the credit terms and the interest rates applied to local borrowers.

Against this benefit, though, there may be a cost if foreign banks are only interested in large firms. Smaller firms may not meet the rules of thumb it applies to borrowers, and the local banks may be left with less credit-worthy borrowers. The possible crowding out of weaker local borrowers may require policies designed to help the local financial sector adjust. The objective would be to ensure that marginal borrowers could continue to secure credit through regional development or risk capital societies.

The key issue, though, for the poorer countries and regions is whether they can take advantage of EMU to accelerate their development. We have already seen that Spain and Portugal have reaped considerable benefits from EC membership and the move to 1992. It is quite possible, as we have argued elsewhere, that business confidence will receive a similar sort of boost from the move to EMU. In these circumstances, the change in monetary regime – from separate national currencies to a single European one – could radically lift the growth path of the poorer regions. If the Community's growth accelerates, it is likely that the poorer regions will accelerate by more. As we have seen, the poorer regions do better relatively when the environment is better absolutely.

There is another reason why the poorer regions might be expected to gain disproportionately from EMU, more than offsetting any putative losses from the abandonment of a separate currency and exchange rate changes. This is simply that businesses would, in some cases for the first time, have considerable confidence in the stability of the macro-economic environment. Negligible inflation, low interest rates, and a fixed exchange rate would all be attractive.

9 The views of the European countries

So far, we have looked at the overall costs and benefits which could be expected to flow from EMU. We have also looked at the possible impact on poorer regions. This stress on the overall impact is correct because, above all, EMU is a change whose benefits should outweigh its costs for all the participants. It is not a zero-sum game in which one group gains what another group loses, but a positive-sum gain in which all can win.

Nevertheless, there is understandable interest in the distribution of costs and benefits through the member states if only because some elements of the negotiation of EMU will substantially affect who wins most. It is quite consistent to point out that everyone can win, and also to have member states arguing for a larger share of the gains by means of a lower contribution or higher receipts through any redistribution of resources through the budget.

The obvious approach, taken in the first part of each country summary below, is to see how the different conditions in each economy make it more or less likely to be affected by particular costs or benefits. A table at the end of the chapter gives some key economic indicators for each of the member states. The second part of each country section deals with points made in the national debates in political and opinion-forming circles. These positions are only partly formed, since at the time of writing the debate was only getting under way. Many of the views also represented an opening position in a prolonged negotiation during the inter-governmental conference which began on December 14th, 1990. Another table at the end of the chapter gives details of the public opinion polls undertaken by Eurobarometer in each of the member states.

The countries are grouped according to the extent of their participation in the European Monetary System: narrow banders, broad banders, and non-participants. Countries that are already fixed closely to the German mark, and whose inflation rates are similar, have already paid the major costs of EMU. What remains are the benefits. The countries whose currencies are less aligned, and whose inflation rates are higher, have greater benefits in store but larger transitional costs to overcome as well. For small, very open economies, the benefits are particularly clear cut. If they have currencies which are not much used internationally, they will also pay high transactions costs.

Another important consideration is the extent to which the anti-inflationary credibility of national economic institutions would be improved by EMU. This is a source of gain for most countries with a record of high inflation and interest rates. The fact that an independent Euro-fed is more likely to be believed when it says it will control inflation means that wage-bargainers and businessmen are less likely to adopt inflationary wage and price behaviour. This is not merely a gain when the economy has to adapt to some shock, but it is also potentially a gain in moving to EMU.

On all these counts, the major exception is Germany, because the Bundesbank already has anti-inflationary credibility in abundance. The major potential benefits of EMU for Germany are different. As a large exporter of goods and capital to other Community countries, Germany has a large interest in their macroeconomic stability.

1 Countries with currencies in the narrow band of the exchange rate mechanism

Germany
Benefits and costs

Germany has the largest surplus of exports over imports in the Community, a position which leads it to build up claims on the assets of foreign countries. These overseas investments are an increasingly important source of revenue, and also play a role in ensuring that the pensions and social security payments which will have to be paid to an ageing German population can be met. Without a cushion of foreign investment and earnings, the impost on younger generations of Germans would be very burdensome.

Germany's overseas investments are thus crucial. For German investors, EMU will remove the macroeconomic risk that their assets will fall in value in terms of Deutschmarks because of a devaluation of the currency in which they have invested, or that nominal amounts will be eroded by overseas inflation. By contrast, Germany could not expect to benefit particularly from the reduction in transactions costs, because a sizeable proportion of German trade is already denominated in Deutschmarks.

Nor would Germany benefit from the anti-inflationary credibility of the Euro-fed. Indeed, the reverse may happen even if the Euro-fed's independence of political control is enshrined more formally than the Bundesbank's, since it is arguable that the Euro-fed will find it hard to inherit the Bundesbank's reputation at once. But there will nevertheless be some gains for Germany on the monetary front. The reinforcement by EMU of the commitment to price stability in Germany's neighbours inevitably means that there is less risk of imported inflation. Germany will be able to avoid the exchange rate pressures which accompany the development of the Deutschmark into a reserve currency, a trend which would be likely to continue with the liberalisation of Eastern Europe.

Germany's own economic and monetary union is also having repercussions in Europe as a whole. It is likely to cause some increase in demand, inflation, and imports for a while. Interest rates are thus also likely to be higher than otherwise, although this may in time be mitigated if the federal government reduces its own demands on national savings by raising taxes or introducing offsetting cuts in spending to make way for the new commitments in the east. This increase in German inflation is likely to mean an even closer convergence of economic performance with the rest of the Community, albeit as a result of a deterioration in Germany rather than an improvement elsewhere.

German views

The Federal government has given strong support to the objective of economic and monetary union and to the broad approach proposed in the Delors report. It sees economic advantages in EMU, but it also sees it as a necessary step in the process of European integration to which the Federal Republic has long been committed. Within the Christian Democrat/Christian Social Union side of the coalition, there are some differences of nuance between the Chancellor's enthusiastic position and the more sceptical views of the Finance Minister, Mr Theo Waigel. Mr Hans-Dietrich Genscher, the Foreign minister and leader of the Free Democrats, is a staunch supporter of the Delors approach.

Not surprisingly, the Bundesbank has struck a more cautious position than the Government not least, perhaps, because its own prerogatives are subsumed by a proposed Euro-fed. In its September 1990 "Statement on the establishment of an economic and monetary union in Europe", the Bundesbank remains very much in favour of the "coronation theory" – the view that EMU must result only as the final stage of a prolonged period of convergence of key economic variables (notably inflation) and institutional safeguards. It argues that "substantial transitional problems as a result of the intra-German unification process" and the uncertainties in Eastern Europe justify postponement of any further steps to EMU "until such time as the economic situation in Germany as a whole and in the European Community can be regarded as sufficiently consolidated".

Once progress is resumed, in the Bundesbank's view, the member states will have to meet several pre-conditions about economic convergence and the conduct of monetary and fiscal policies. These "can only be fulfilled in the course of a lengthy transitional process. During this process, no institutional changes which result in any curtailment of the freedom of reaction of national monetary policy may be made." In other

monetary policy must be clearly set by only one insti-
There must be no muddying of the waters by means
ransitional stage in which several institutions have a
hana.

Academic opinion is less favourable to EMU than other
opinion-formers in Germany. The Board of Academic
Advisers, a group of thirty academics which advises the economics ministry, has rejected the "coronation theory" but it
has criticised the Delors report because of the process of
transition. It argues that there would be a danger that the
transitional arrangements could become permanent, without
the proper establishment of a fully independent central bank.
Secondly, the economic and financial affairs council would
acquire a weight incompatible with the autonomy of national
central banks. It also doubted the Delors report's proposals
for formal co-ordination and binding rules for fiscal policy.

The Council of Economic Advisers, in its annual report
released in November 1989, said that the Delors report provided a good basis for further discussion, but there were
serious objections to some of its positions. It acknowledged
the advantages of a single currency, but argued that for the
time being the member states' economies were too dissimilar
for them to abandon separate currencies without running
grave risks. Once the 1992 programme had culminated in the
creation of the single market, and there was greater convergence of both nominal variables like inflation and real variables like living standards, the conditions for monetary union
would improve.

The Eurobarometer survey taken in the autumn of 1989
suggested that German public opinion is mildly in favour of
EMU. It is attracted by the advantages of a single currency for
private transactions.

France
Benefits and costs

EMU will consolidate France's close convergence with Germany's economic performance since the middle eighties. Pegging French monetary policy to an anti-inflationary standard

as well entrenched as that of the Bundesbank should dispel any remaining doubts in the markets about France's intentions. Interest rates will tend to decline as the perceived exchange rate risk of holding francs is eliminated and a continuation of France's low rate of inflation becomes more credible. This process will improve the public finances by reducing the servicing cost of public debt. Lower interest rates, together with savings in transactions costs and the elimination of exchange rate risk, will encourage an expansion of private investment.

France will thus be a prime beneficiary of EMU in terms of its effects on perceptions of future inflation and stability. The commitment to EMU may also help to persuade people to adapt their own behaviour, particularly in setting pay costs. The inflexibility of the labour market, perhaps in part due to the failure of wage bargainers to recognise the anti-inflationary shift of French government policy in recent years, has been an important cause of the persistent problem of relatively high unemployment.

France should also benefit from the waning of the constraints imposed on growth by the current account of the balance of payments, which has been a long-standing preoccupation of French policy makers. EMU will create an environment where free capital flows will be more willing to finance current account deficits, because of the commitment to low inflation and a fixed exchange rate. Both effectively remove the macroeconomic risks of overseas investment. During the transition, smaller interest rate differentials will be needed to produce the necessary capital flows. Thereafter, the constraint will be lifted entirely.

An additional benefit for France is that it will have a representative on the board of the Euro-fed, which may make anti-inflationary policy more acceptable politically. At present, it has no influence over Bundesbank policy, which is determined wholly by anti-inflationary concerns within Germany. A Euro-fed will give equal weight to the domestic demand and inflationary pressures in France and other participating members of EMU.

French views

The Government favours moving rapidly to EMU for both political and economic reasons. It is widely accepted in France that devaluing the franc is no longer a helpful means of reducing the current account deficit. The implicit transfer of monetary sovereignty from a national to a pan-European monetary authority is accepted. Indeed, it is regarded as advantageous by comparison with a position where the Bank of France has no influence over the decisions made by the Bundesbank which effectively determine its own monetary policy.

The French government also, importantly, supports the proposition that the Euro-fed should be independent of the political process. The only caveat concerns budgetary policy, where the Ministry of Economy and Finance has voiced its concern about the binding rules proposed by the Delors report. There are few differences of nuance between the Finance Ministry and the Bank of France. Not surprisingly, the Bank has also declared itself in favour of the independence of the European monetary institution, and Mr Jacques de Larosiere, the Governor, has also argued that a common monetary policy should be directed towards price stability.

Overall, the French authorities have reiterated their strong support for EMU. This has become even stronger, if anything, as a result of the democratisation in Eastern Europe and the reunification of Germany in 1989-90. A long-standing goal of France's foreign policy has been to bind Germany into Western Europe by means of economic integration and a common system of European law for settling disputes. EMU is a logical extension of traditional French policy.

The French political parties in opposition have differing views on EMU. The centre-right UDF grouping led by former President Valery Giscard d'Estaing is in favour of EMU. However, the Gaullist RPR is not in favour of a single European currency, though there is a significant minority which disagrees with this view. For the RPR leadership, a common currency alongside the existing national currencies would be enough to help the single market work effectively. It would also avoid national governments losing their monetary sovereignty.

In academic circles, there is broad support for EMU. Surveys of the heads of large French companies show that they attach great importance to the creation of a single currency. Public opinion, according to the Eurobarometer polls, is also strongly in favour of a single currency.

Italy
Benefits and costs

The Italian lira fluctuated within the wide 6 per cent EMS bands for ten years, and only adopted the narrow 2.25 per cent bands in 1989. Moving to EMU is thus a more dramatic change than it is for France or the other more long-standing members of the narrow EMS band. Although Italy has made immense economic strides in recent years, its performance is still significantly worse than that of other narrow band members in two respects: inflation and the public deficit. These outstanding problems imply that Italy will have to pay higher costs during the transition to EMU. Enormous political courage will be required if taxes are to be raised enough to reduce the public sector deficit.

Nevertheless, Italy also stands to reap larger potential gains if EMU accelerates the process of convergence. It could expect lower inflation, lower interest rates, healthier public finances, and positive effects on the expectations of wage bargainers which might reduce the level of unemployment needed to stabilise wage inflation.

The reduction in interest rates would be particularly important for Italy, because its public sector debt is so high at 98 per cent of national income and because of the present wide margin between Deutschmark and lira interest rates. A decline of 3 percentage points in the treasury bill rate – the gap between German and Italian one year rates in December, 1990 – is calculated to save roughly 9,000 billion lire in the first year ($7.9 billion) and 21,000 billion lire in the second ($18.5 billion).

Lower interest rates will thus significantly reduce the debt service component of the budget deficit, but this alone will not be enough to restore the public finances. Italy's budget deficit was worth 10.2 per cent of national income in 1989, and a concerted effort will be needed to bring the deficit down to a sustainable level. Moreover, two developments associated with EMU will worsen Italy's budget position. The first is the loss of above average seigniorage revenue as the mandatory requirement on banks to hold cash is reduced. The second is the reduction in the withholding tax on the interest paid on bank deposits, which is currently 30 per cent. These losses are not negligible, but they will be more than offset by the gain from lower interest rates. In addition, Italy will participate in the seigniorage gains made by the Euro-fed.

Italian views

The Italian government is a forthright proponent of EMU, and is anxious to move as rapidly as possible to stage three and a single currency. It also stresses the need to bring the budget deficit under control as a discipline necessitated by the moves to EMU.

The Banca d'Italia supports both the principle of EMU and the three-stage process outlined in the Delors report. It welcomes the prospect of a common monetary policy aimed at stable prices, and would like independent status for the Euro-fed. It also favours binding budget rules.

Academic opinion in Italy strongly favours EMU, which it sees as the logical culmination of the process of fixing exchange rates and reducing Italy's inflation. Some scholars have expressed reservations about the premature loss of seigniorage revenue while the public debt is so large. Others are concerned that the less prosperous regions of Italy may be disadvantaged by the loss of the exchange rate as a way of adjusting their competitiveness.

Public opinion broadly supports EMU. This includes business, despite recurrent complaints from industrialists about worsening competitiveness. The public assesses EMU, over and above its economic merits, as part of the process of

European integration. Eurobarometer surveys show that the Italians favour common European policies, including a single currency, by a wider margin than any other nation in the Community.

Belgium
Benefits and costs

The smaller countries within the narrow bands of the EMS have largely paid the costs involved in adjusting to EMU, and have now to reap the benefits. The main benefit for Belgium will be the elimination of exchange rate uncertainty and transaction costs, together with the discipline which EMU can impose on occasionally unruly public finances.

As a relatively small Community economy, possessing a relatively little used currency, Belgium can expect to benefit disproportionately from the reduction in transaction costs as it uses the ecu instead of the Belgian Franc. We have already seen that smaller economies like Belgium's can expect to gain some 1 per cent of national income from the reduction of transaction costs, whereas large member states with currencies which are extensively used in international trade might expect only 0.2 per cent.

Any reduction in interest rates as a result of a greater anti-inflationary credibility should significantly lower the Belgian budget deficit, which was 6.3 per cent of national income in 1989. Belgium has made enormous efforts to curb its public finance problem, but its public debt stands at a high 135 per cent of national income. It thus stands to gain disproportionately from any reduction in interest rates.

Belgian views

The Belgian government has supported both the objective of a single currency and the Delors Report's three stage proposals. The transfer of powers to a supra-national authority is not viewed as lessening national sovereignty, since Belgium is perceived to have little autonomy in monetary policy in any case. Opposition parties accept the principle of EMU but question the Government's ability to deal with the problems of the public finances.

Netherlands
Benefits and costs

Dutch inflation is now slightly lower than that in Germany, and the guilder has remained fixed against the Deutschmark for many years. It has therefore paid the transitional costs of reducing inflation, and has merely to reap the benefits of EMU.

This will mean lower transactions costs. As in the case of Belgium, the reduction of transaction costs will be of particular benefit to the Netherlands because it is a small economy with a currency little-used in international trade.

The budget deficit, though, is still a sizeable 5.1 per cent of national income (in 1989) and the public debt is a high 83 per cent of GDP. Both need to be reduced to ensure that the Netherlands will have the freedom of manoeuvre in budgetary policy which may be necessary to cushion shocks within EMU.

Dutch views

The Dutch government has supported EMU. There is a widespread view that it is in the Netherlands' interest that monetary decisions should be taken by a Community body and not monopolised by the larger Community countries. The Government shares this view, and also stresses the importance of the principle of subsidiarity. The Social and Economic Council has favoured an independent central bank for Europe, along German lines. Academic opinion supports a single currency.

Luxembourg
Benefits and costs

EMU will have a particular impact on Luxembourg, if only because of the importance of the financial sector within the economy. There will be two offsetting effects. Capital market liberalisation and the abolition of exchange rate uncertainty should benefit Luxembourg as a financial centre, but the introduction of common rules for EC banks could undermine some of the advantages of using Luxembourg as a base for operations. A single currency will also tend to diminish the volume of banking business generated by the foreign exchanges, currency arbitrage, and tax evasion.

Luxembourgeois views

The Luxembourgeois government supports the three stages outlined in the Delors report. The Government's reservations concern the transfer of sovereignty over budgetary policy. The Ministry of Finance expects integration to intensify, but it fears that a Treaty revision might lead to the abandonment of unanimous decision-making over tax policy.

Denmark
Benefits and costs

Denmark might gain less than other small countries within the narrow band of the EMS from the removal of transaction costs and uncertainty, simply because a larger proportion of its trade is with other Nordic countries which are not members of the Community. (On the other hand, the deepening integration with the EC of these Nordic countries is increasingly drawing them towards applications for membership.)

EMU will bring particular benefits in terms of public finances, because Denmark is relatively highly indebted and can be expected to pay a lower interest rate within EMU because of the anti-inflationary credibility of an independent Euro-fed. The current account constraint, which has historically been important to Denmark, would also be lifted.

Danish views

The Economics ministry supports full participation by Denmark in the process of EMU as set out by the Delors report. It sees advantages in a single currency rather than merely locking exchange rates, but is concerned that subsidiarity should be applied, particularly in fiscal policy. The Central bank favours a gradual movement towards EMU, emphasising that growing interdependence has reduced the room for manoeuvre even of medium-sized economies. Participation in the Euro-fed is seen to offer Denmark more influence over its monetary policy than it has at present.

There has also been a marked change recently in the attitude of the opposition Social Democratic party. At a meeting of European Socialists in Dublin in May 1990, they took a more positive approach to the Community in general and to EMU.

Ireland
Benefits and costs

Ireland has made a lot of progress in reducing both wage and price inflation, and in cutting its budget and external deficits. Much of the adjustment needed to move to EMU has thus been achieved. EMU will help to ensure that these achievements are sustained, and will make Ireland even more attractive to foreign investment by eliminating exchange rate uncertainties.

The weaknesses of the Irish economy are low income per head, high unemployment and emigration. There is heavy reliance on agriculture, and much of industry remains inefficient. EMU would thus represent a considerable challenge to Ireland, as well as an undeniable opportunity.

A further cut in the Ireland's debt – which stands at 104 per cent of national income – is essential. Clearly, the lower interest rates which are likely within EMU will help. But an additional margin is necessary if Ireland is to be able to use budget policy to offset the impact of any economic shocks.

Irish views

The Government supports the principle of EMU, but it stresses the need for the Community to take account of the objective to strengthen economic and social cohesion set out in Article 130(a) of the amended Treaty. This is also the position of the main opposition parties. The particular concern in political circles is that EMU might have adverse effects on the ability of a peripheral, small and less technologically advanced economy to compete. There are also worries about the impact of EMU on the national budget if it requires a similar tax base.

Nevertheless, there is a general consensus in favour of EMU in Ireland. A report produced by the National Economic and Social Council in 1989 broadly represented the combined viewpoints of the administration, the trade unions, the employers and agricultural interests. It concluded that the Community should aim to create an advanced economic and monetary union, on the basis that a succesful EMU required a substantial budgetary redistribution to poorer regions and countries.

The Governor of the Central Bank echoed these concerns when he argued, in a paper to the Delors committee, that EMU would only be feasible if all regions of the Community had reached a similar level of development. He recommended more Community policies to that end.

2 Countries with currencies in the broad band of the exchange rate mechanism

Spain
Benefits and costs

Spain, which only recently became a member of the exchange rate mechanism, is in a situation similar to that of other Community countries when they first joined. The top priority is to use the ERM to curb inflation and the external deficit. But this means that the roles of monetary and fiscal policy have to change. With monetary policy increasingly directed to maintaining the peseta within its bands, often by lower rates of interest than might be required if monetary policy were directed solely to the control of domestic demand. This conflict between two objectives – the target of the exchange rate and the control of domestic demand – can be resolved by a tighter budget policy.

Spain is one of the countries which might benefit particularly from the credibility of an independent Euro-fed in affecting price and wage expectations. Any reduction in interest rates would also help Spain cut its budget deficit, which is meant to reach balance by 1992 and which stood at 2 per cent of national income in 1989. In addition, Spain has benefited enormously from the inflow of direct investment in the wake of its EC membership. This could be expected to continue and intensify as more foreign businesses decided to take advantage of low labour costs now that exchange rate uncertainty was eliminated.

Spanish views

The Spanish government is in favour of closer economic and monetary integration but would like this to include help for less developed regions of the Community. The Minister of Economy and Finance, Carlos Solchaga, sees no reason why accepting the exchange rate discipline of the EMS should put a brake on medium term growth prospects, which would be better balanced if inflation slowed. However, he is wary of proceeding rapidly towards monetary union. By contrast, Prime Minister Felipe Gonzalez is for a rapid move. The Governor of the Central Bank has supported monetary union and its implications.

Business leaders also assess the EMU process very positively, preferring some loss of national independence in economic policy-making to the fluctuations in the policy mix that has often occurred in the past. They also favour an independent central bank.

Academic opinion believes that EMU will have beneficial effects by obliging Spain to adopt a restrictive fiscal policy, and to reintroduce an incomes policy. Many add that it should be complemented by appropriate measures of regional policy. Some academics, though, believe that EMU could have adverse effects on Spain because of the loss of the exchange rate as a means of adjusting to changes in the world economy and correcting the external deficit during a rapid period of catching-up.

Public support for EMU is strong and increasing. Spanish public opinion, according to Eurobarometer, is second only to Italy's in favouring a common monetary policy.

Britain
Benefits and costs

Britain is, in several respects, just beginning the process of economic convergence on which other Community countries embarked in 1979. The sharp boom at the end of the eighties has left the economy seriously out of balance. Even the underlying inflation rate has been running at double that of the narrow band ERM countries. The external deficit, reflecting a prolonged period during which domestic demand outstripped supply, is large and unsustainable. This unfortunate experience, after a period of earlier success in reducing inflation, has undermined the Government's own credibility in dealing with inflation.

It may take some time for the Government to recoup its standing with both the financial and the labour markets. As a result, the financial markets may continue to require a high level of interest rates in order to offset the perceived risk of a depreciation, while wage bargainers may continue to demand high pay settlements in order to offset the perceived risk of inflation. These reactions may in turn mean that there is a period of severe output and employment losses.

If, though, Britain succeeds in reducing its inflation rate sharply, it should be able to draw particular benefits from EMU. An independent Euro-fed would avoid the problems of lost credibility which the monetary authorities in Britain have suffered, and could in time improve the relationship between unemployment and inflation. The external constraint which has bedevilled British economic policy for much of the post-war period would be eased by the availability of overseas funding.

The City of London remains Europe's pre-eminent financial centre, and could expect to become the hub of the development of the Europe-wide equity, bond and money markets if Britain adopts a single currency. Britain has also benefited disproportionately from American and Japanese investment in the Community, thanks to access to the Community market, low labour costs and the English language. If there were an investment boom as a result of EMU, Britain would once again prove to be a disproportionate beneficiary. But if Britain does not participate in EMU, it is likely that the position of the City and the high share of foreign investment would be eroded. For Britain, there can thus be disproportionate gains from EMU. But Britain is also in an unusual position among the member states in that it might actually suffer losses if it were to fail to participate in EMU.

British views

The British government committed itself to economic and monetary union at the Hanover summit in 1988, as it had done on several occasions in the past. At the Madrid summit in June 1989, it also committed itself to stage one of the Delors report, during which sterling would participate within the ERM. The so-called "Madrid conditions" for full British membership included lower inflation and free capital movements.

Opposition to sterling's membership of the ERM, both within the government and from academic opinion, centred on the monetarist view that policy should be directed at pursuing explicitly domestic objectives, notably the control of the monetary aggregates. This viewpoint weakened as the Government found increasing difficulty in controlling the money supply, and as different measures of money contradicted each other. Sterling was put into the ERM on 8 October 1990.

This did not, though, imply acceptance of stages two or three of the Delors report. The British government has instead proposed the establishment of a 'hard ecu', a thirteenth currency in addition to the Community's existing twelve. It would be run by a European Monetary Fund as a member of the European Monetary System, but on the principle that its parity could never be devalued compared with any other currency in the system. It should thus always be the strongest currency in the system, and be the most attractive to investors. As a result, its interest rate would effectively form a floor below which other currencies' interest rates would not fall. In order to avoid any net increase in money creation which could be inflationary, national central banks would be under an obligation to repurchase holdings of their own currency which had been sold to the EMF.

Eventually, this system could develop into one of fixed exchange rates, or the "hard ecu" could become a substitute for national currencies "if governments and peoples so choose" as Prime Minister John Major has said. The British government is not in favour of rapid moves to a single currency, although it will participate in the negotiations about the statutes of any central bank designed to operate it. A substantial body of opinion within the House of Commons, particularly on the Conservative side, regards monetary policy as an important element of national sovereignty.

The Bank of England, after an initially favourable attitude in part due to the participation in a personal capacity on the Delors commitee of the governor, now sees virtues in the Treasury's proposals for a "hard ecu". It does, however, favour its own independence as a central bank, a principle which, of course, is widely supported for a European central bank.

The Labour Party, Trades Union Congress and the Confederation of British Industry all now back economic and monetary union in the form of a single currency. However, the CBI sees a single currency as coming only after a successful process of convergence, while the Labour party and the TUC advocate the democratic accountability of the Euro-fed and a more extensive system of regional funding.

The opinion of academic economists and the institutes is more mixed, with a majority, but not an overwhelming one, in favour of a single currency. There is criticism of the Delors report's proposals for binding budget guidelines.

3 Countries with currencies outside the exchange rate mechanism

Greece
Benefits and costs

Attempts to close the gap between the Greek and the Community economy have met with limited success. Inflation was close to 14 per cent in 1989, and accelerated to more than 20 per cent in the first half of 1990. The budget deficit amounted to 18 per cent of national income in 1989, a very large amount even after taking account of the element due to high nominal interest rates at a time of high inflation. The public debt stood at 105 per cent of national income in 1989. Living standards have also slipped from 58 per cent of the Community average in 1980 (at purchasing power parities, which allow for differences in prices) to 54 per cent in 1989.

The decision of the centre-right government not to devalue to the full extent of the gap between Greece's rise in prices and that of its partners, combined with a restrictive wage policy and a programme to halve the budget deficit by 1993, should ensure that inflation comes down and so pave the way for participation in the exchange rate mechanism. Full membership of the EMS would then reinforce the credibility of Greece's efforts to keep inflation down.

Greece might benefit from a leap to EMU, which would be rather similar to a currency reform. So long as the problem of the public sector deficit was tackled decisively, inflationary expectations would be dealt a mortal blow, and might provide Greece with a shortcut to what might otherwise prove to a long and painful process of disinflation. This strategy may be particularly appropriate given that the major problem with disinflation is not the rigidity of Greek labour markets, which are relatively ununionised, but the lack of credibility of the Greek monetary authorities.

Given Greece's low labour costs, a stable macroeconomic environment could dramatically encourage inward foreign investment. Such capital flows would also ease the external constraint on Greek growth and help to reinvigorate the battered confidence of the private sector.

Greek views

Most academic, business and political opinion favours progress towards EMU and Greece's eventual participation. However, there are also considerable worries about the readiness of the Greek economy for the full rigours of competition without the protection of a separate currency. The new government has nevertheless expressed its determination to implement its economic programme, which envisages Greece being able to join the ERM by 1993.

Portugal
Benefits and costs

The Portuguese economy has made some progress towards convergence with the rest of the Community since its membership in 1986. Inflation has fallen from 19 per cent in 1985 to 13 per cent in 1989. The public finances remain weak, but they have improved slightly. In 1989, the budget deficit was worth 5 per cent of national income and the public debt stood at 70 per cent of national income. Further cuts in the deficit will be necessary before Portugal can realistically participate in the ERM and the EMU. Otherwise, similar considerations must apply to Portugal as apply to Greece.

Portuguese views

The Portuguese government supports the principle of EMU and the three stage proposals of the Delors report. But it has also argued that EMU risks widening the gap between Portugal and the more developed member states. To minimise the costs and risks for Portugal, EMU should be accompanied by an increase in the Community's structural funds. The Portuguese authorities have said that the escudo should join the ERM relatively soon, but that the present large inflation differential between Portugal and the core ERM countries is 9 per cent, which prevents any move in the near future.

Among politicians, there is broad but qualified support for

joining the ERM and for EMU. Business is worried about the possible deterioration in Portuguese competitiveness, particularly in traditional export sectors like textiles and footwear where there is mounting competition from the newly industrialising countries. There is also a concern about the loss of control of domestic companies to foreign capital.

Most of those in the academic community who favour ERM membership believe that the escudo should participate only when Portuguese inflation is nearer to the EC average, but some believe that membership would provide a reinforcement for the counter-inflationary effort.

Table 23 Selected economic indicators for EC member states 1980-89

	B	DK	D	GR	E	F	IRL	I	L	NL	P	UK	EC 12
GDP per capita (EC=100)													
1980	104,2	108,1	113,8	58,2	73,4	111,8	64,1	102,6	116,0	111,1	55,1	101,1	100
1989	102,3	106,5	112,7	54,2	75,8	108,8	67,1	103,7	125,8	103,0	55,0	106,3	100
Private consumption deflator (Annual percentage change)													
1980	6,4	10,7	5,8	21,9	16,5	13,3	18,6	20,4	7,6	6,9	21,6	16,2	13,5
1989	3,1	5,0	3,1	13,8	6,6	3,5	4,1	6,0	3,4	1,1	12,8	5,8	4,8
General government lending (+)/borrowing (−) (As % of GDP)													
1980	−9,2	−3,3	−2,9	:	−2,6	0,0	−12,7	−8,6	−0,4	−4,0	:	−3,4	:
1989	−6,3	−0,7	0,2	−17,6	−2,1	−1,3	−3,1	−10,2	3,3	−5,1	−5,0	1,6	−2,8
Intra-EC trade (as % of GDP)													
Imports													
1980	36,0	14,9	11,4	10,9	5,0	10,6	43,5	10,2	36,0	24,8	17,1	9,1	12,2
1989	45,4	14,1	11,9	15,2	10,2	13,8	36,6	10,1	45,4	30,0	27,0	12,2	14,2
Exports													
1980	38,5	13,2	12,1	6,4	5,1	9,3	33,5	8,9	38,5	32,1	10,8	9,6	12,3
1989	46,3	13,5	15,7	6,9	7,8	11,9	47,3	9,2	46,3	37,0	19,5	9,3	14,2

Table 24 Eurobarometer survey, autumn 1989
Unification of Western Europe and decision-making on currency

Unification of Western Europe[1]

	B	DK	D	GR	E	F	IRL	I	L	NL	P	UK	EUR 12
For very much	31	24	42	54	41	29	38	44	32	26	47	27	37
For some extent	54	36	37	28	35	50	33	42	42	50	22	42	41
Against to some extent	6	19	8	3	4	7	4	4	14	11	4	12	7
Against very much	1	14	2	3	2	2	3	1	4	5	1	5	3
No reply	8	7	10	12	18	12	22	9	8	8	26	14	12
Total	100	100	100	100	100	100	100	100	100	100	100	100	100

Decision-making on currency[2]

	B	DK	D	GR	E	F	IRL	I	L	NL	P	UK	EUR 12
Community	67	54	59	44	46	72	57	68	56	53	28	42	57
National	28	38	35	39	39	23	35	24	33	38	49	51	35

Questions

[1] *Attitude towards the unification of Western Europe*
In general, are you for or against efforts being made to unify Western Europe? If FOR, are you very much for this, or only to some extent? If AGAINST, are you only to some extent against or very much against?

[2] *National or joint Community decision-making*
Some people believe that certain areas of policy should be decided by (national) government, while other areas of policy should be decided jointly within the European Community. Interviewees were given a range of policy areas (including currency) and asked to express a view as to the appropriate forum for decision-making.

Glossary of terms

Arbitrage The process of buying or selling goods in order to take advantage of differences in price in two different markets. As arbitrageurs buy in the cheaper market and sell in the dearer one, the price difference narrows.

Asset Something of value held by individual or institution. Financial assets include bonds and shares. A bank's loans are part of its assets.

Asymmetry Changes or shocks are said to affect countries asymmetrically when they affect them in different ways. Symmetrical shocks affect countries in the same way.

Budget deficit/surplus The balance between government spending and government revenues.

Central Bank The institution in any country which has a monopoly over the issue of banknotes and coins. Because it controls the supply of money, it can influence the interest rates people pay. Central banks can be independent of political influence (like the German Bundesbank) or under political control (like the Bank of France and the Bank of England).

Commission The Commission proposes draft Community laws - directives and regulations - to the Council and the EC Parliament, and is responsible for running policies once they are agreed. It also has a judicial function as upholder of the Community Treaties. It can take member states, companies and individuals to the European Court if it believes they are breaching the Treaties. There are 17 Commissioners appointed by national governments. The big countries –

Britain, Germany, France, Italy and Spain – have two. The rest have one each.

Competence The areas over which the Community is competent include trade policy with third countries, the Common Agricultural Policy, and measures to ensure free trade within the Community including the setting of standards. However, Article 235 of the Treaty of Rome gives the Council enabling powers to extend its competence to areas not explicitly covered by the Treaty.

Competitiveness The ability of a country to compete internationally. This depends on non-price factors such as technology, delivery dates and quality. But it also depends on prices and costs. A typical measure of competitiveness shows the movement in wage costs per unit of output in one country compared with another. Rising wages are, of course, a good thing if they are paid for by rising output per person (or productivity). Wage costs per unit of output only rise if wage costs outstrip productivity growth.

A fall in wage costs compared with other countries is a gain in competitiveness, which is also called a fall in the real exchange rate. Similarly, a rise in wage costs per unit of output is a loss in competitiveness, which is also called a rise in the real exchange rate.

Convergence The process of economies becoming more similar in their performance. The term is especially used about inflation rates.

Coronation theory The view that EMU should only come about as the final, crowning moment at the end of the prolonged period of convergence of key economic variables such as inflation and the balance of payments.

Council of Ministers The EC Council is the Community's legislative body. If it approves regulations or directives, they have the status of law subject to some modest approval by the European parliament. The Council is composed of one minister from each of the twelve member states. It meets regularly to discuss different matters of EC concern: the general affairs council is attended by foreign ministers; the economic and finance ministers council by the Chancellor and so on.

Counter-factual case What would have happened in the absence of something, in this case Economic and Monetary Union.

Credibility In an economic context, the credibility of the monetary authorities is crucial in limiting the costs of bringing down inflation. If they tighten policies but businesses and wage bargainers do not believe that they will really bring down inflation, costs and prices will go on increasing, and the company will price itself out of markets.

Current account of the balance of payments The balance between exports of goods and services plus receipts of interest, profits and dividends on overseas investments minus the imports of goods and services plus payments of interest, profits and dividends on foreigners' investment in the country.

Delors report Report into the means of introducing a single currency for Europe drawn up by the Community's central bank governors under the chairmanship of Commission President Jacques Delors.

Devaluation The reduction in value of one currency in terms of others. If the pound sterling is worth 2.95 Deutschmarks, and its value changes to 2.65 Deutschmarks, the pound has devalued by a little more than 10 per cent. A revaluation is when one currency rises in value in terms of others. A devaluation makes the exports of a country cheaper when priced in the currencies of other countries, and makes imports more expensive in the home currency. A revaluation does the opposite.

Disinflation The process of reducing inflation.

Economic union The state in which different national markets for products have no real meaning, since they are merely part of a wider economic union in which prices are effectively the same (after allowing for transport costs) for similar goods. An economic union will have a common framework of competition policy.

Economies of scale The savings which are made from producing more of the same thing, perhaps through spreading overhead costs (like management) over more output or services.

Ecu The ecu or European currency unit is a "basket" currency composed of fixed proportions of different Community currencies, and which therefore reflects their movements. It has no independent value of its own. It is used in Community and private business. If the ecu became the European single currency, it would take on a value of its own regulated by its central bank and the interest rates paid on it. In February 1991, the 'basket' ecu was worth some $1.40.

Efficiency In economic terms, efficiency means producing what people want at the lowest cost. An improvement in efficiency will tend to result in lower prices for consumers.

European Community Twelve member states (Belgium, Britain, Denmark, France, Germany, Greece, Ireland, Italy, Luxembourg, Portugal, the Netherlands, and Spain) which have signed treaties regulating their relationship with each other, and agreeing to operate certain common policies. Its principal institutions are the Council of Ministers, the European Council, the European Parliament, the European Commission, and the European Court of Justice.

European Council A Euro-summit of heads of state and government, like a super-council of ministers. It has no formal constitutional role in the Community, but the junior councils of ministers (for transport, agriculture and so on) tend to take notice.

European Monetary System The EMS is a system of fixed but adjustable exchange rates designed to create a zone of monetary stability in Europe. The exchange rate mechanism of the EMS, in which all community currencies participate except the Greek drachma and the Portuguese escudo, limits movements of a currency to within 2.25 per cent of its target or "central" rate against the ecu and each other ERM currency.

The pound sterling and the Spanish peseta operate a special, wider 6 per cent band of fluctuation.

Exchange rate The rate at which one currency is exchanged for another. Under a fixed but adjustable system like the European Monetary System's exchange rate mechanism, the rate is rarely changed. Under monetary union, it is fixed for all time.

Exchange rate mechanism *see* European Monetary System.

Exogenous Outside the economic system; unaffected by other things going on within the system.

External deficit *see* Current account of the balance of payments.

Factor mobility The mobility of factors of production (workers, physical investment in plant and machinery).

Fiscal drag The phenomenon whereby inflation raises more government revenue because tax thresholds are not indexed to price rises.

Fiscal policy The policy towards the balance of taxation and public spending. An expansionary fiscal policy (or stance) involves cutting taxes or increasing public spending, and moving from surplus towards (or into greater) deficit. A contractionary fiscal policy involves raising taxes or cutting public spending, and moving from deficit towards surplus or greater surplus.

Fiscal transfers Cash taken from rich regions to give to poor ones.

Fiscal stance *see* Fiscal policy.

Game theory The study of the interaction of small groups, which is particularly important in assessing the outcome of co-operation or conflict.

G3/G5/G7 The various groups of leading industrial countries which meet to co-ordinate their policies. G3 is Germany, Japan and the United States; G5 adds Britain and France; G7 adds Canada and Italy.

Gross Domestic Product The value of all the goods and services produced in an area in a given time, usually a year. It can be called national income, output or expenditure. All should add up to the same amount. GDP plus net interest, profits and dividends from or to overseas adds up to Gross National Product (GNP).

Inflation The rise in the average price level over time.

Inflation tax The revenue which a government receives from issuing banknotes at a time of high inflation. Governments always benefit from some seigniorage revenue - the revenue gained by the issue of currency – and this tends to rise at a time of inflation as people have to hold more money.

Inter-governmental conference (IGC) Conferences of national governments which began in Rome on December 14, 1990: designed to agree a new treaty of political union and a new treaty on economic and monetary union.

Liquid A market is liquid when it is possible to buy and sell in it. Assets are liquid when they can be readily turned into cash. Cash is the most liquid asset.

Macroeconomics That part of economics which deals with the behaviour of the economy as a whole system, rather than with the behaviour of individual parts of an economy such firms or consumers (which is micro-economics).

Microeconomics *see* Macroeconomics.

Monetary union This can be defined as the irrevocable fixing of exchange rates for different currencies, whereby one pound, say, will always be exchanged for the same number of German marks. Or it can be defined as a single currency to replace all the existing twelve currencies. In economic terms, there is little difference between the two. The Commission prefers a single currency, even with different designs on each country's banknotes, because people would believe there was less risk of breaking the link.

National income *see* Gross domestic product.

Nominal Confusingly, economists refer to things as nominal when they are as they are to be found in the real world, as distinguished from real things which only exist in economists' minds: these are nominal things after allowing for inflation. A 10 per cent increase in nominal demand is the amount by which demand actually went up in money terms. If prices rose by 8 per cent, the change in real demand - nominal demand after allowing for inflation - was only 2 per cent.

Non-accomodating policy Interest rate and tax and public spending policies which aim to slow down the growth of total spending in the economy (or money demand) and hence to stop price rises. If inflation responds slowly, as it generally does, the real spending in the economy also slows down, which depresses output growth.

Open Open to trade and hence also to external influences. A relatively open economy is an economy a high proportion of whose output is exported, and of whose sales are imported. Luxembourg is a very open economy, and Japan is not.

Organisation for Economic Co-operation and Development (OECD) Paris-based intergovernmental organisation of the developed economies devoted to research and exchange of ideas.

Price competitiveness *see* Competitiveness.

Productivity Output per person or output per person-hour.

Progressive As applied to a tax system, this means that a higher proportion of income is paid in tax if people are better off.

Purchasing power parity The rate of exchange between two or more countries which would equalise their average price level. Research undertaken by the Commission and the OECD compiles price lists for different economies so that their real living standards - after allowing for price differences - can be compared.

Real *see* Nominal.

Real exchange rate *see* Competitiveness *and* Nominal.

Regulation *see* Directive.

Reserve requirement/ratio Banks hold a certain proportion of their deposits in ready cash or near-cash (such as deposits at a central bank) in order to ensure that they are able to pay out whatever depositors demand. This is usually a legal requirement.

Revaluation *see* Devaluation.

Schengen group Originally five countries - Germany, France and the Benelux - which agreed to abolish border controls and establish common visa and other requirements. Now joined by Italy, they represent the six original member states of the Community, arguably the most committed to growing together.

Seigniorage revenue *see* Inflation tax.

Single European Act 1985 The Single Act was a new EC Treaty, simplifying the former Treaties and re-establishing the principle of voting by majority in the Council of Ministers on issues to do with the creation of the single european market - the 1992 programme.

Subsidiarity A principle which holds that decisions ought to be taken as near to the people affected by them as possible, unless there are compelling reasons, on grounds of efficiency, for doing otherwise.

Stages one, two, three The stages set out in the Delors report (see above) for the move to EMU. See Chapter 1.

Standard deviation A commonly used measure of the degree to which a variable is spread (or dispersed) around its mean (average) value.

Sticky wages or prices The phenomenon whereby prices or wages react only very slowly to a change in economic conditions such as a fall in demand.

Symmetry *see* Asymmetry.

Variable Something that changes or varies, such as growth or the inflation rate or consumers' spending.

Select bibliography

Abraham, F. (1989), *Wage norms and Europe's single market*,
International Economics Research Paper 63, Centrum voor
Economische Studién, Katholieke Universiteit Leuven.

Aglietta M. (1988), "Regimes Monetaires, Monnaie Supranationale,
Monnaie Commune". Communication á la Conférence
International de Barcelona sur la théorie de la régulation, June
1988.

—— Coudert V., and Delessy H. (1990), "Politiques budgétaires et
adjustements macro-économiques dans la perspective de
l'intégration monétaire européenne", in *Lectures critiques du rapport
Delors*, De Pecunia vol II, n2-3, Brussels, September.

Aizenman J. and Frenkel J.A. (1985), "Optimal Wage Indexation,
Foreign Exchange Intervention, and Monetary Policy", *American
Economic Review*, vol75 n3, June.

Akerloff G. and Yelen J. (1989), "Rational Models of Irrational
behaviour", *American Economic Review*, May.

Alogoskoufis G. and Portes R. (1990), "International Costs and
Benefits from EMU", in Commission of the EC (1990a).

Argy V. (1989), "Choice of Exchange Rate Regime for a Smaller
Economy – A Survey of Some Key Issues", Paper prepared for the
CEPS/IMF Conference on Exchange Rate Policy in Selected
Industrial Economies, Brussels, October.

Artis M. (1989), "The Call of a Common Currency" in *Europe Without
Currency Parities*, S. Brittan and M. Artis, Social Market
Foundation, London 1989.

—— and Bayoumi T. (1989), *Saving, investment, financial integration
and the balance of payments*, IMF Working Paper 89/102, International
Monetary Fund, Washington, DC, December 14.

—— and Taylor U. (1988) "Exchange Rate, interest rates, capital
controls and the European Monetary System: assessing the track
record" in *The European Monetary System*, F. Giavazzi, S. Micossi
and M. Miller, eds. Banca d'Italia/CEPR.

Backus and Drifill (1985), "Inflation and Reputation", American Economic Review, June.

Balassa B. (1961), *The theory of economic integration*, Richard Irwin, New York.

—— (1964), "The purchasing power parity doctrine: a reappraisal", *Journal of Political Economy*, December.

Baldwin R. (1989), "The Growth Effects of 1992", *Economic Policy*, October.

—— (1990), "On the Microeconomics of EMU", in Commission of the EC (1990a).

—— and Krugman P. (1987), "The Persistence of the U.S. Trade Deficit", Brookings Papers on Economic Activity n1.

—— and Lyons R. (1990), "External Economics and European Integration: The Potential for Self-Fulfilling Expectations", in Commission of the EC (1990a).

Barenco B. (1990), "The Dollar Position of the Non-US Private Sector, Portfolio Effects, and the Exchange Rate of the Dollar", OECD Working Paper n76, February.

Barro R.J. and Gordon D. (1983), "A Critical Theory of Monetary Policy in a National Rate Model", *Journal of Political Economy*, 91, 589-610, August.

Bayoumi T.A. (1989), *Saving-investment correlations: immobile capital, government policy or endogenous behaviour?*, IMF Working Paper 89/66, International Monetary Fund, Washington, DC, August 22.

—— and Rose A.K. (1989), *Domestic savings and intra-national capital flows*, Mimeo, December.

Begg D. (1990), "Alternative exchange rate regimes: the role of the exchange rate and the implications for wage-price adjustment", in Commission of the EC (1990a).

Bekx P., Bucher A., Italianer A., and Mors M. (1989), "The Quest Model (version 1988)", EC Economic papers n75, March.

Bertola G. (1988), "Factor Flexibility, uncertainty and exchange rate regimes", in M. De Ceccho and A. Giovannini, *A European Central Bank?*, Cambridge University Press, Cambridge.

BEUC – Bureau Européen des Unions de Consommateurs (1988), "Transferts d'argent à l'intérieur de la C.E.E.", April.

—— (1988b), "Holiday Money", July.

Bhandari J. and Mayer T. (1990), *Saving-investment correlation in the EMS*, Mimeo, January.

Bini-Smaghi (1987), *Exchange Rate Variability and Trade Flows*, Mimeo, University of Chicago and Banca d'Italia, 1987.

Black S. (1985), "International Money and International Monetary

Arrangements", in *Handbook of International Economics*, volume II,
R.W. Jones and P.B. Kenen, eds., Elsevier Science Publishers B.V.
—— (1989), "Transaction Costs and Vehicle Currencies",
International Monetary Fund Working Paper, November.

Blanchard O.J. and Fisher S. (1989), *Lectures on Macroeconomics*, MIT
Press, Cambridge, Massachusetts.

Bliss C. and Braga de Macedo J. (1990) *Unity with diversity within the
European economy: the Community's Southern Frontier*, Cambridge
University Press, Cambridge.

Blundell-Wignall A. and Masson P. (1985), "Exchange rate dynamics
and intervention rules", *IMF Staff Papers* vol 32, March.

Bofinger P. (1990), "Economic Reform in Eastern Europe:
Implications for the Ecu, the EMS, and European Monetary Union",
Paper for the Conference "Vers L'Union Economique et Monétaire",
organized by the Ministére de l'Economie, des Finances et du
Budget, Paris, June.

Borts (1960) "The equalization of returns and regional economic
growth", *American Economic Review*, 50: 319-347.

Boyd C., Gielens G. and Gros D. (1990) *Bid/ask Spreads in the Foreign
Exchange Markets*, Mimeo, Brussels, February.

Braga de Macedo J. (1990), "External liberalization with ambiguous
public response: the experience of Portugal", in Bliss C. and Braga
de Macedo J. (1990).

—— Goldstein, and Meerschwan (1984), "International Portfolio
Diversification", in *Exchange Rate Theory and Practice*, Bilson and
Marston, eds.

Brandsma A. and Hughes, Hallett A. (1989), "The Design of
Interdependent Policies With Incomplete Information", *Economic
Modelling*, July.

Brandsma A. and Pijpers J.R. (1985), "Co-ordinated Strategies for
Economic Cooperation between Europe and the United States",
Weltwirtschaftliches Archiv, Heft 2.

Branson W. (1990), "Financial market integration, macroeconomic
policy and the EMS" in *Economic Integration in the Enlarged E.C.*, Braga
de Macedo and Bliss, eds., Cambridge University Press, Cambridge.

Brender A., Gaye P., and Kessler V. (1986), "L'après-dollar",
Economica, Paris.

Buigues P., Ilzkovitz F., and Lebrum J. F. (1990), "Les Etats membres
face aux enjeux sectoriels du marché intérieur", *European Economy*
n44 and *Social Europe*.

Byé M. (1958) "Localisation de l'investissement et communauté
économique européenne", *Revue Economique*.

Canzoneri M. and Gray J.A. (1985), "Monetary Policy Games and the Consequences of non-cooperative behaviour", *International Economic Review* vol26 n3, October.

Canzonieri M. and Rogers C.A. (1989), "Is the European Community an Optimal Currency area? Optimal Taxation versus the cost of Multiple Currencies", *American Economic Review*, November.

Calmfors L. and Driffill J. (1988), "Centralization of wage bargaining", *Economic Policy* 6, April, pp13-61.

Carli G. (1989) "The Evolution towards Economic and Monetary Union: A Response to the HM Treasury Paper", Ministerio del Tesoro, December.

CEPII and OFCE (1990), "MIMOSA, une modélisation de l'économie mondiale", Observations et diagnostics économiques 30, Observatoire Français des Conjonctures Economiques, Paris, January.

Chevassus E. (1989), "Le choix de la monnaie de facturation", thése de doctorat, Université de Paris X Nanterre.

Clark C., Wilson F., and Bradley J. (1969) "Industrial location and economic potential in Western Europe", *Regional Studies*, 2.

Coe D.T. (1985), "Nominal wages, the NAIRU and wage flexibility", *OECD Economic Studies* 5, Autumn, pp87-126.

Cohen D. and Wyplosz C. (1989), "The European monetary union: an agnostic evaluation", in *Macroeconomic policies in an Interdependent World*, R.C. Bryant, D.A. Currie, J.A. Frenkel, P.R. Masson, R. Portes, eds., International Monetary Fund, CEPR/IMF and Brookings Institution, pp311-337.

Commission of the EC (1977), Report of the study group on the role of public finance in European integration, Collection studies, Economic and financial series Nos. A13/B13, Commission of the EC, Brussels/Luxembourg, April.

—— (1987), Third periodic report on the social and economic situation and development of the regions of the Community, Commission of the EC, Luxembourg.

—— (1988), "The economics of 1992", *European Economy* 35, Commission of the EC, Luxembourg, March.

—— (1989), *Communication from the Commission concerning its action programme relating to the implementation of the Community Charter of basic social rights for workers*, COM (89) 568 final, Brussels, 29 November.

—— (1990a), "One market, one money", *European Economy* 44, October, Luxembourg.

—— (1990b) "The economic and financial situation in Germany", Economic Papers.

Confederation of British Industry (1989), "European Monetary Union: A Business Perspective", London, November.

Cooper R. (1984), "A Monetary System for the Future", Foreign Affairs, Fall.

Council of Ministers (1990), "Décision du Conseil relative à la réalisation de convergence progressive des politiques et des performances économiques pendant la première étape de l'Union économique et monétaire", in Economie Européenne, Supplément A n3, March.

Cukierman A. (1983), "Relative price variability and inflation: a survey and further results" Carnegie-Rochester Conference series on public policy 19.

—— (1990), "Fixed parities versus a commonly managed currency and the case against 'stage two'", Ministry of Finance, Paris, June 21.

Currie D., Holtham G. and Hughes, Hallett A. (1989), "The Theory and Practice of International Policy Co-ordination: Does Co-ordination Pay?", in Macroeconomic Policies in an Interdependent World, R.C. Bryant, D.A. Currie, J.A. Frenkel, P.R. Masson, R. Portes, eds., International Monetary Fund, CEPR/IMF and Brookings Institution.

De Grauwe R. (1987), "International trade and economic growth in the European Monetary System", European Economic Review, 31, 389–398.

De Jonquières G. (1990), "Counting the costs of dual pricing in the runup to 1992", Financial Times.

Dealtry M. and Van't dack J. (1989), "The US External Deficit and Associated Shifts in International Portfolios", BIS Economic Papers, n25, September.

Dixit A. (1989), "Entry and Exit Decisions under Uncertainty", Journal of Political Economy, 1989, vol97, pp. 620-630.

Donges J. (1986), Whither International Trade Policies? Worries about Continuing Protectionism, Institut für Weltwirtschaft, Kiel.

Dooley, Lizondo, Mathieson (1989), "The Currency Composition of Foreign Exchange Reserves", IMF Staff Papers, vol 36, n2, June.

Dornbusch R. (1980), Open economy macroeconomics, Basic Books, New York.

—— (1989), "Credibility, debt and unemployment: Ireland's failed stabilization", Economic Policy 8, pp. 173-209.

—— (1990), *Problems of European Monetary Integration*, MIT Press, Cambridge, Massachusetts

Driffill J. (1989), "The stability and sustainability of the European Monetary System with perfect capital markets", in *The European Monetary System*, F. Giavazzi, S. Micossi and M. Miller, eds., Banca d'Italia/CEPR.

Edison, Hali J. (1990), "Foreign Currency Operations: An Annotated Bibliography", International Finance Discussion Paper n 380, Board of Governors of the Federal Reserve System, May.

Eichengreen B. (1989), "Hegemonic Stability Theories of the International Monetary System", in *Can Nations Agree? Issues in International Economic Cooperation*, R. Cooper, B. Eichengreen, C. Randall, G. Holtham and R. Putnam, eds., The Brookings Institution, Washington.

—— (1990), "One money for Europe? Lessons from the US currency union", *Economic Policy* 10, April, pp117-187.

Emerson M., Aujean M., Catinat M., Goybet P., and Jacquemin A. (1988), *The economics of 1992*, Oxford University Press.

—— (1988), "The Economics of 1992", *European Economy* n35.

Engle R.F. and Granger C.W.J. (1987), "Co-integration and error-correction: representation, estimation and testing", *Econometrica* 55 n2, March, pp251-276.

European Economy (1988), "Creation of a European financial area", Special issue n36, May.

Eurostat (1989), *Basic statistics of the Community*, Commission of the EC, Luxembourg.

Faini R. (1990) "Regional development and economic integration: the case of Southern Italy', paper presented at the conference "Portugal and the Internal Market of the EC", Lisbon.

Fair R.C. (1988), "Sources of economic fluctuations in the United States", *Quarterly Journal of Economics*, May, pp313-332.

Feldstein M. (1988), "Distinguished Lecture on Economics in Government: Thinking About International Economic Coordination", *Journal of Economic Perspectives*, vol 12, Spring.

—— and Bacchetta P. (1989), "National saving and international investment", National Bureau of Economic Research paper presented at conference on saving.

—— and Horioka C. (1980), "Domestic saving and international capital flows", *Economic Journal* 90, June, pp314-329.

Fischer S. (1981), "Towards an understanding of the costs of inflation: II'' Carnegie-Rochester Conference series on public policy 15, 5-42.

Flood R., Bhandari J. and Horne J. (1989) "Evolution of Exchange Rate Regimes", *IMF Staff Papers*, vol36, n4, December.

Frankel J. (1982), "In search of the exchange rate premium: a six currency test assuming mean variance optimization", *Journal of International Money and Finance* vol 1, pp 255-274, December.

—— (1986), "The implications of Mean-Variance Optimization for Four Questions in International Macroeconomics", *Journal of International Money and Finance* vol 5, March.

—— (1988), "Obstacles to International Macroeconomic Policy Coordination", *Princeton Studies in International Finance*, University of Princeton.

—— and Rockett K. (1988), "International Macroeconomic Policy Coordination When Policymakers Do Not Agree on the True Model", *American Economic Review* vol 78, June.

Frenkel J.A. (1989), "Quantifying international capital mobility in the 1980s", NBER Working Paper n2856, National Bureau of Economic Research, Cambridge, Massachusetts, February.

—— Goldstein M. and Masson P.R. (1989), "Simulating the effects of some simple coordinated versus uncoordinated policy rules", in *Macroeconomic Policies in an Interdependent World* R.C. Bryant, D.A. Currie, J.A. Frenkel, P.R. Masson and R. Portes eds., International Monetary Fund, CEPR/IMF and Brookings Institution, pp. 203-239.

—— and Razin A. (1987), *Fiscal policies and the world economy*, MIT Press, Cambridge Massachusetts.

Friedman M. (1953), "The Case for Flexible Exchange Rates", in *Essays in Positive Economics*, University of Chicago Press.

Fuller W.A. (1976), *Introduction to statistical time series*, John Wiley, New York.

Funabashi Y. (1988), *Managing the Dollar: From the Plaza to the Lonne*, Institute for International Economics, Washington.

Gagnon J. (1989), "Exchange Rate Variability and the Level of International Trade", Board of Governors of the Federal Reserve System, International Finance Discussion Paper n369, December 1989.

Gandolfo (1987), *International Economics*, Springer Verlag, Berlin/ Heidelberg.

Genberg H. (1989), "In the Shadow of the Mark: Exchange Rate and Monetary Policy in Austria and Switzerland", Paper presented to the CEPS-IMF Seminar on "Exchange Rate Policy in Selected Industrial Economies", Brussels, October.

Giavazzi F. and Giovannini A. (1987), "Exchange rates and prices in Europe", *Weltwirtschaftliches Archiv* 124 n4, pp592-604.

—— (1989), "Monetary Policy Interactions under Managed Exchange Rates", *Economica* 56, 199-213.

—— (1989), *The European Monetary System*, MIT Press, Cambridge, Massachusetts.

Giavazzi F. and Spaventa L. (1990), "The 'New' EMS", CEPR Discussion paper n 369, January

Giavazzi F. and Pagano M. (1988), "The Advantage of Tying One's Hands", *European Economic Review*, June.

Giersch H. (1949), "Economic union between nations and the location of industries", *Review of Economic Studies* 17, pp87-97.

Giovannini A. (1989), "How do fixed-exchange rate regimes work? Evidence from the gold standard Bretton Woods and the EMS", *Blueprints for Exchange Rate Management*, January.

Greenaway D. and Milner C. (1986), *The economics of intra-industry trade*, Basil Blackwell, Oxford/New York.

Gros D. (1987), "Exchange Rate Variability and Foreign Trade in the Presence of Adjustment Costs", Working Paper n8704, Département des Sciences Economiques, Université Catholique de Louvain, Louvain-la-Neuve.

—— (1989), "On the Volatility of Exchange Rates – A Test of Monetary and Portfolio Models of Exchange Rate Determination" *Weltwirtschaftliches Archiv*, June 1989, pp273 – 295.

—— (1990), "EMS without capital controls", *Ecu Newsletter*, n30, pp. 22-26, October.

Heller and Knight (1978), "Reserve-Currency preferences of Central Banks", *Essays in International Finance*, Princeton University.

—— (1986), "An Analysis of the Management of the Currency Composition of Reserve Assets"

Helpman and Krugman (1985), *Market Structure and Foreign Trade*, MIT Press, Cambridge, Massachusetts.

Hochreiter and Türnqvist (1990), "Austria's Monetary and Exchange Rate Policy, Some Comparative Remarks with Respect to Sweden," in *Lectures critiques du rapport Delors*, De Pecunia vol II n2-3, Brussels, September.

Holtfrerich C.L. (1989), "The monetary unification process in nineteenth-century Germany: relevance and lessons for Europe today", in *A European Central Bank?*, M. De Cecco and A. Giovannini, eds., IPMG/CEPR/Cambridge University Press.

Horn H. and Persson T. (1988), "Exchange rate policy, wage

formation and credibility", *European Economic Review* 32 n8, October, pp1621-1636

Hughes, Hallett A. (1986), "Autonomy and the Choice of Policy in Asymmetrically Dependent Economics", *Oxford Economic Papers* vol38.

IFO-Institut für Wirtschaftsforschung (1989), *An empirical assessment of factors shaping regional competitiveness in problem regions*, Munich.

Ingram C. (1973), "The Case for European Monetary Integration", *Princeton essays in International Finance*, n98, Princeton University, April.

International Monetary Fund (1984) "Exchange rate variability and world trade", *Occasional paper* n28, IMF.

Ishiyama Y. (1975), "The Theory of Optimum Currency Areas: A Survey", *IMF Staff Papers* vol22.

Jacquemin A. and Sapir A. (1988), "International trade and integration of the European Community: An econometric analysis", *European Economic Review* 32, n7, September, pp1439-1449.

Katseli, L. (1990), "Economic Integration in the enlarged European Community: structural adjustment of the Greek economy" in Bliss C. and Braga de Macedo J. (1990).

Keeble D., Offord J., and Walker S. (1988), *Peripheral regions in a Community of twelve member states*, Commission of the European Communities, Brussels.

Kenen P.B. (1969), "The Theory of Optimum Currency Areas: an Eclectic View", in *Monetary Problems of the International Economy*, R.A. Mundell and P. Kenen, eds.

—— (1983), "The Role of the Dollar as an International Currency", *The Group of Thirty, Occasional Papers* 13, New York.

Keohane R.O. (1984), *After Hegemony*, Princeton University Press.

Kindelberger (1973), *The World in Depression, 1929–1939*, University of California Press, Berkeley.

Kiyotaki N. and Wright R. (1989), "On Money as a Medium of Exchange", *Journal of Political Economy*, vol97, n4, August.

Krugman P. (1980), "Vehicle Currencies and the Structure of International Exchange", *Journal of Money, Credit and Banking*, August.

—— (1984), "The International Role of the Dollar: Theory and Prospect", in *Exchange Rate Theory and Practice*, J.F.O. Bilsen and R.C. Marston, eds., University of Chicago Press/NBFR.

—— (1989a), "Is Bilateralism Bad?", NBER Working Paper n 2972, May.

—— (1989b), *Exchange Rate Instability*, MIT Press, Cambridge, Massachusetts.

—— (1989c), "Policy Problems of a Monetary Union", paper prepared for the CEPR/Bank of Greece Conference on "The EMS in the 1990s".

—— (1989d), "Differences in income elasticities and trends in real exchange rates", *European Economic Review* 33, pp1031-1054.

—— (1989e), "Increasing returns and economic geography", NBER Working Paper, Washington.

—— and Venables A. (1990), "Integration and the competitiveness of peripheral industry", in Bliss C. and Braga de Macedo J. (1990).

Kydland F.E. and Prescott E.C. (1977), "Rules Rather than Discretion: The Inconsistency of Optimal Plans", *Journal of Political Economy*, vol85, n3.

Lamfalussy A. (1989), "Macro-coordination of fiscal policies in an economic and monetary union in Europe", in *Committee for the study of economic and monetary union, Report on economic and monetary union in the European Community*, Commission of the EC, Luxembourg, pp91-125.

Lebégue D. (1985), "Pour une réforme du systéme monétaire international", *Economie Prospective Internationale*, n24, 4ème trimestre 1985.

Lucas R.E. (1976), "Econometric Policy Evaluation: A Critique", in *The Phillips Curve and Labor Markets*, K. Brunner and A.H. Meltzer, eds., Carnegie-Rochester Conference Series on Public Policy 1, pp19-46.

McKinnon R.I. (1963), "Optimum Currency Areas", *American Economic Review*, vol53, pp 717-725, September.

—— (1988), "Monetary and Exchange Rate Policies for International Financial Stability: A Proposal", *Journal of Economic Perspectives*, vol2 n1, winter.

Magnifico G. (1973), *European monetary unification*, Macmillan, London.

Marsden D. (1989), "Occupations; The influence of the unemployment situation", in *Wage differentials in the European Community*, W.T.M. Molle and A. van Mourik, eds., Avebury/ Gower, Aldershot, pp105-139.

Marston R.C. (1984), "Exchange Rate Unions as an Alternative to

Flexible Rates: The Effects of Real and Monetary Disturbances", in *Exchange Rate Theory and Practice*, J.F. Bilson and R.C. Marston, eds., NBER/University of Chicago Press.

—— (1985), "Stabilization policies in open economies", *Handbook of international economics*, vollII, R. Jones & P. Kenen, eds., Elsevier Science Publishers.

Masson P. and Melitz J. (1990), "Fiscal policy independence in a European Monetary Union", Paper prepared for a conference on "Exchange rate regimes and currency unions", Deutsche Bundesbank, February 21-23.

Masson P., Symansky S., Haas R., and Dooley M. (1988), "MULTIMOD – A multi-region econometric model", *World economic and financial surveys*, International Monetary Fund, Washington, DC, April, pp50-104.

Meade J.E. (1957), "The Balance-of-Payments Problems of a European Free- Trade Area", *Economic Journal*, vol.67, pp 379-396, September.

Meese R. and Rogoff K. (1983), "Empirical Exchange Rate Models of the Seventies: Do they fit out of Sample", *Journal of International Economics* 1983 pp3-24.

Molle W.T.M. and van Mourik A. (1988), "International migration of labour under conditions of economic integration: the case of Western Europe", *Journal of Common Market Studies* 26, pp369-394.

Molle W.T.M. (1989), "Will the completion of the internal market lead to regional divergence?", paper presented at the conference 'The completion of the internal market', Kiel, June 1989.

Mundell (1961), "A Theory of Optimum Currency Areas", *American Economic Review*, September.

Mussa M. (1986), "Nominal Exchange Rate Regimes and the behaviour of real exchange rate: Evidence and Implications", *Carnegie Rochester Series on Public Policy*, pp117 – 214.

Myrdal G. (1957), *Economic theory and underdeveloped regions*, Duckworth London.

Neumann M. and von Hagen J. (1989), "Conditional relative price variance and its determinants: open economy evidence from Germany", *International Economic Review*, February 1991.

Neven D. (1990), "EEC integration towards 1992: some distributional aspects", *Economic Policy*, April 1990.

Obstfeld M. (1989), "Competitiveness, Realignment, and Speculation: the Role of Financial Markets", in *The European Monetary System*, F. Giavazzi, S. Micossi and M. Miller, eds., Banca d'Italia/CEPR.

OECD (1989), *Regional policy developments in OECD countries*, Paris.
—— (1989a), *Economies in transition*, OECD, Paris.
—— (1989b), *National Accounts*, vol II, 1975-1987, OECD, Department of Economics and Statistics, Paris.
—— (1990), *Italy*, OECD Economic Surveys, Paris.
Oi W.Y. (1961), "The Desirability of Price Instability Under Perfect Competition", *Econometrica*, vol29, n1, January, pp58-64.
Oliveira-Martins J. and Plihon D. (1990), "Transferts internationaux d'épargne et intégration financière", *Economie et Statisque*.
Ondiz G. and Sachs J. (1984), "Macroeconomic Policy Coordination among the Industrial Economics", *Brooking Papers on Economic Activity*.

Padoa-Schioppa T. (1987), *Efficiency, Stability, Equity*, Oxford University Press, Oxford.
Perée E. and Steinherr A. (1989), "Exchange Rate Uncertainty and Foreign Trade", *European Economic Review*, 33, pp1241-1264.
Perroux F. (1959), "Les formes de concurrence dans le marché commun", *Révue d'économie politique*, 1.
Persson and Svenson (1987), "Exchange Rate Variability and Asset Trade", presentated at the Conference "Exchange Rate Variability", Toronto, September 1987.
Pindyck R. S. (1982), "Adjustment Costs, Uncertainty and the Behavior of the Firm", *American Economic Review*, June 1982, n72, pp415-427.
Poloz S. (1990), *Real Exchange Rate Adjustments between Regions in a Common Currency Area*, Mimeo, Bank of Canada, February.
Putnam R. and Bayne N. (1987), *Hanging Together: Cooperation and Conflict in the Seven Power Summits*, Harvard University Press.

Richardson P. (1987), *A review of the simulation properties of OECD's INTERLINK model*, OECD Working Paper 47, OECD, Economics and Statistics Department.
Romer P. (1986), "Increasing returns and long-run growth", *Journal of Political Economy*, October, n94, pp1002-37.
—— (1989), "Increasing returns and new developments in the theory of growth", NBER Working paper n 3098, September.

Sachs J. and and Sala-i-Martin X. (1989), *Federal fiscal policy and optimum currency areas*, Mimeo, Harvard University.
Sapir A. and Sekkat K. (1989), *Exchange Rate Variability and International Trade: The Effects of the European Monetary System*,

Mimeo, Université Libre du Bruxelles.

Sargent T.J. (1987), *Macroeconomic theory* (2nd edition), Academic Press, London.

Schultze C.L. (1985), "Real wages, real wage aspirations, and unemployment in Europe", in *Barriers to European Growth*, R.Z. Lawrence and C.L. Schultze, eds., The Brookings Institution, Washington, DC, pp230-291.

Scitovski T. (1958), *Economic theory and Western European integration*, Stanford University Press.

Sneessens H.R. and Dréze J.H. (1986), "A discussion of Belgian unemployment", *Economica* 53, ppS89-S119.

Stahl H. M. (1974), *Regionalpolitische Implikationen einer EWG-Währungsunion*, Tübingen.

Tavlas G.S. (1990), "On the International Use of Currencies: The Case of the Deutsche Mark", IMF Working Paper WP/90/3, January.

Tootell G.M.B. (1990), "Central bank flexibility and the drawbacks to currency unification", *New England Economic Review*, Federal Reserve Bank of Boston, May/June, pp 3-18.

Ungerer H., Evans O., Mayer T., and Young P. (1986), "The European Monetary System: Recent Developments", *Occasional Paper* no. 48, International Monetary Fund, Washington, DC, December.

Van der Ploeg (1990), "Macroeconomic Policy Coordination during the Various Phases of Economic and Monetary Integration in Europe", in Commission of the EC (1990a).

Van Rompuy P., Abraham F., and Heremans D. (1990), "Economic federalism and the EMU", in Commission of the EC (1990a).

Van Rompuy V. and Heylen E. (1986), *Openbare financién in de deelgebieden van federale landen* (Public finance in the regions of federal countries), Acco, Leuven.

Vanhove N. and Klaassen L. H. (1980) *Regional policy: a European approach*, Saxon House.

Viéals J. et al. (1990), "Spain and the EC cum 1992 shock" in *Economic Integration in the Enlarged E.C.*, J. Braga de Macedo and C. Bliss, eds., Cambridge University Press.

Walters A. (1990), "Sterling in danger", Institute of Economic Affairs, London.

Weber A.A. (1990), "Asymmetries and adjustment problems: some empirical evidence", in Commission of the EC (1990a).

Wihlborg C. and Willett T. (1990), *Optimum Currency Areas Revisited*, Mimeo, April.

Williamson J. (1965), "Regional inequality and the process of national development: a description of the patterns", *Economic development and cultural change*, n13, pp3-45.

—— (1985), *The Exchange Rate System*, Institute for International Economics, Washington.

—— and Miller M. (1987), *Targets and Indicators: A Blueprint for the International Coordination of Economic Policy*, Institute for International Economics, Washington.

Wyplosz C. (1990), "Monetary union and fiscal policy discipline", in Commission of the EC (1990a).

Zenezini M. (1989), "Wages and unemployment in Italy", *Labour* 3 n2, pp57-99.

Index

All Pan books are available at your local bookshop or newsagent, or can be ordered direct from the publisher. Indicate the number of copies required and fill in the form below.

Send to: **CS Department, Pan Books Ltd., P.O. Box 40,**
             Basingstoke, Hants.   RG21 2YT.

or phone: 0256 469551 (Ansaphone), quoting title, author
             and Credit Card number.

Please enclose a remittance* to the value of the cover price plus: 60p for the first book plus 30p per copy for each additional book ordered to a maximum charge of £2.40 to cover postage and packing.

*Payment may be made in sterling by UK personal cheque, postal order, sterling draft or international money order, made payable to Pan Books Ltd.

Alternatively by Barclaycard/Access:

Card No. | | | | | | | | | | | | | | | | |

Signature:

Applicable only in the UK and Republic of Ireland.

While every effort is made to keep prices low, it is sometimes necessary to increase prices at short notice. Pan Books reserve the right to show on covers and charge new retail prices which may differ from those advertised in the text or elsewhere.

NAME AND ADDRESS IN BLOCK LETTERS PLEASE:

....

Name————————————————————————

Address————————————————————————

————————————————————————

————————————————————————

————————————————————————

3/87